Weber's® Little Barbecue Book™

matthew drennan

photography chris alack

MQP

Published by MQ Publications Ltd.
12 The Ivories, 6–8 Northampton Street
Tel: +44 (0)20 7359 2244
Fax: +44 (0)20 7359 1616
email: mail@mqpublications.com
website: www.mqpublications.com

Editorial Team:
Managing Editor: Ljiljana Ortolja-Baird
Editors: Abi Rowsell and Marsha Capen
Photography: Chris Alack
Food styling: Carol Tennant and Matthew Drennan
Illustrations: Marc Dando
Recipe credits: Matthew Drennan; Sunset Books, Inc.;
Weber®'s Art of the Grill™, published by Chronicle Books,
© Weber-Stephen Products Co.; and the Cookbook
at weber.com
Photographic credits: Weber-Stephen Products Co.; p.6
(bottom left), p.78 / Stephen Hamilton, p.14

The material in this book has been adapted from
Weber®'s Ultimate Barbecue Book™.

Produced by MQ Publications Ltd under exclusive
licence from Weber-Stephen Products Co.

MQ Publications:
Zaro Weil, CEO & Publisher

Weber-Stephen Products Co.:
Mike Kempster Sr., Executive Vice President
Jeff Stephen, Vice President Export Sales
Marsha Capen, Director of Marketing

Heatbeads® is a registered trademark of
Australian Char Pty Ltd.

A CIP catalogue record for this book is available
from the British Library

ISBN: 1-84072-482-X

Printed in France by **Partenaires-Livres®** (jl)

1 3 5 7 9 8 6 4 2

Contents

Barbecue basics

This chapter introduces you to the ease of setting up, lighting and using your charcoal or gas barbecue, including what kind of fuel to use and how much charcoal to use on your grill. It describes both the Direct and Indirect cooking methods, giving you flexibility in barbecuing. You can learn how to use your grill to suit the food you are planning to cook, from a simple chicken breast to a leg of lamb. Cooking and safety guidelines are provided, as well as advice on barbecue accessories, and tips on how to keep barbecuing simple and fun.

Many of the recipes in the book use delicious marinades, rubs and flavoured butters to enhance the food and lock in flavour. Tried and tested recipes for these are featured in each chapter, most of which can be made in advance.

Charcoal grills

The secret of cooking on a charcoal kettle lies in the proper use of the lid and the air damper system, along with two proven methods of positioning the charcoal briquettes. Cold air is drawn through the bottom vents to provide the oxygen necessary to keep the coals burning. The air heats and rises and is reflected off the lid, so it circulates around the food being cooked, eventually passing out through the top vent. Thus a kettle grill cooks in the same manner as a convection oven, making it ideal for roasts and whole poultry, in addition to the more common steaks and sausages.

The temperature is always higher at the start of cooking and as the coals burn down the temperature will gradually fall. For Indirect cooking, adding coals every hour will maintain a consistent grilling temperature (see chart on page 9).

How to light your charcoal grill

1 Remove the lid and open all of the air vents before building the fire.

2 Spread the charcoal over the charcoal grate (this is the heavy grate at the bottom of the kettle), then pile it into a mound in the centre of the grate. Spreading the charcoal over the grate first helps you determine how much you will actually need.

3 Insert 4 firelighters (see **figure 1**).

4 Light the firelighters and let the coals catch alight and burn (see **figure 2**) until they are covered with a light grey ash. This usually takes about 25–30 minutes. You can also use a chimney starter (see the note on page 6). Then, using tongs arrange the coals on the grate according to the cooking method you are going to use: the Direct or Indirect method. Finally, place the cooking grate over the coals. The grill is now ready (see **figure 3**).

figure 1

figure 2

figure 3

Lighting agents

■ Firelighters

Barbecue firelighters are waxy-looking cubes or sticks, which are designed to light the barbecue without giving off any harmful fumes that could taint the food. Push four into the charcoal and light with a taper or a long stem match. They are easy to use, clean and safe. Only use firelighters designed for barbecues. Do not use firelighters designed for domestic fires as they will contain paraffin, which will spoil the food.

■ Firelighter fluid

If using this product you should handle with care. It should be sprayed on the dry coals, left for a few minutes to soak in, then ignited with a taper or long stem match. Never spray on hot or burning coals because the flames can travel up into the bottle causing serious burns.

Chimney starter

A metal canister with a handle, a chimney starter holds a supply of charcoal. Crumpled newspaper or firelighters are put on the charcoal grate and lit, the chimney starter filled with coals is positioned over the firelighters. The walls of the chimney starter focus the flames and heat onto the charcoal, thereby decreasing the amount of time it takes for the coals to light and ash over. Once the coals are ready, simply tip the coals onto the grate and arrange them for grilling as shown in *figures 4* and *7*.

Direct cooking

This method of grilling is recommended for foods that take less than 25 minutes to cook through, such as steaks and kebabs. Remember to always cook with the lid on for best results.

1 First, prepare and light the charcoal grill as demonstrated on page 5, then spread the coals in an even layer across the charcoal grate (see **figure 4**).

2 Place the food on the cooking grate, cover with the lid and cook directly over the heat source (see **figure 5**). The heat cooks the food from directly underneath (see **figure 6**). The food should always be turned once halfway through the recommended grilling time.

figure 4

figure 5

figure 6

Indirect cooking

This method is recommended for roasts, ribs, whole poultry and other large cuts of meat which take longer than 25 minutes. Remember to always cook with the lid on for best results.

1 First, prepare and light the charcoal grill as demonstrated on page 5 and then arrange the coals evenly on each side of the charcoal grate using charcoal rails or baskets to stabilize. Place a foil drip pan in the centre of the grate between the burning coals (see **figure 7**). This prevents flare-ups particularly when cooking fatty foods and it's useful for collecting drippings, for gravies and sauces.

2 Place the food in the centre of the cooking grate, cover with the lid and cook Indirectly (see **figure 8**). The heat rises around the food, reflecting off the inside surfaces of the kettle, and cooks the food evenly on all sides (see **figure 9**). This circulating heat works like a convection oven, so there is no need to turn the food. Charcoal briquettes will need to be added each hour to maintain a constant roasting temperature (see chart on page 9).

figure 7

figure 8

figure 9

Charcoal fuel

There are many different brands of charcoal but there are only two main types, charcoal briquettes and lumpwood. Lumpwood burns hotter and faster than briquettes.

■ **Charcoal briquettes** These are even sized lumps of fuel made from particles of charcoal mixed with a starch binder. They tend to burn longer than lumpwood charcoal. There are two types of briquettes that you can use – the larger, traditional squarish ones, and smaller round ones that are also known as Heatbeads®. These burn somewhat faster than traditional briquettes – consult the chart opposite for comparisons. It is a good idea to count the briquettes you use. After a while, you will become familiar with the quantity required and you will be able to judge it visually. Use the chart opposite to determine how many briquettes you require, depending on the type used.

■ **Lumpwood charcoal** This is not fossilized fuel extracted from the ground like coal, but is in fact wood that has been fired in a kiln. The process burns the wood without setting fire to it and drives out all the by-products, leaving behind a very light black combustible form of carbon. Opt for good quality brands, which give you larger pieces that light easier and burn better and are less likely to fall through the charcoal grate as they burn down. Instant lighting lumpwood charcoal is also available, which has been impregnated with a lighting agent and comes in a sealed paper bag. The whole bag is placed in the barbecue and ignited.

Because this type of charcoal requires wood from trees for its manufacture, unregulated deforestation became a concern as the world-wide popularity of barbecuing increased. There is now an internationally-known organisation called the Forest Stewardship Council (FSC) which is sponsored by the World Wildlife Fund that monitors and regulates the use of trees from selected areas of forest. Look for charcoal with the FSC logo.

How many briquettes you need to use

BBQ kettle	Square traditional briquettes	Round charcoal beads
37cm (14½ inches) diameter	15 each side	12–24 each side
47cm (18½ inches) diameter	20 each side	28–56 each side
57cm (22½ inches) diameter	25 each side	44–88 each side
95cm (37½ inches) diameter	75 each side	4–8kg each side
Charcoal Go-Anywhere®	15 each side	12–24 each side

How many briquettes you need to add per hour for Indirect cooking

BBQ kettle	Number of coals per side / per hour
37cm (14½ inches) diameter	6
47cm (18½ inches) diameter	7
57cm (22½ inches) diameter	8
95cm (37½ inches) diameter	22
Charcoal Go-Anywhere®	6

▶ Woody herbs such as rosemary can be scattered on the hot coals just before cooking to add flavour to the food.

The barbecue recipes in this book are graded for ease of use with the following symbols:

Recipe symbol	Meaning
✳	Simple
✳ ✳	Moderate
✳ ✳ ✳	Advanced

Key to method of cooking

In the following fish, poultry, meat, vegetable and fruit grilling charts on pages 23, 39, 57, 79 and 99 the approximate cooking time is followed by the barbecue method, as below. These methods are also referred to throughout the book.

DL	Direct Low heat
DM	Direct Medium heat
DH	Direct High heat
IM	Indirect Medium heat
IH	Indirect High heat

Gas grills

Gas grills have one main advantage over charcoal and that's speed. Once your gas bottle is attached it's as simple as turning on the convection oven in your kitchen. Simply flick the ignition switch and within about ten to fifteen minutes the barbecue is up to heat and ready to use.

Gas barbecues are run on Liquid Petroleum (LP) gas which comes in two forms, butane or propane. The gas is under moderate pressure in the cylinder and is liquid. As the pressure is released the liquid vaporizes and becomes a gas.

How to light your gas grill

1 Check there is enough fuel in your tank (some grills have gauges to measure how much gas is in the tank). Check to see all the burner control knobs are turned off. Open the lid.

2 Turn the gas valve on the bottle to 'on'.

3 Turn on one burner and light the grill according to the manufacturer's directions using either the ignition switch or a match. When the gas flame has ignited, turn on the other burners.

4 Close the lid and preheat the grill until the thermometer reads 500–550°F, 245–275°C. This takes about 10–15 minutes. Then adjust the burner controls according to the cooking method, Direct (see **figure 10**) or Indirect (see **figure 12**), you are going to use. The grill is now ready for cooking.

■ **Always read the safety instructions carefully on transporting, storing and fitting gas bottles.**

Direct cooking

This method of grilling is recommended for foods that take less than 25 minutes to cook through, such as steaks and kebabs. Remember to always cook with the lid on for best results.

1 Ignite the grill, and turn all burners onto High, close the lid and leave to come up to heat. Adjust the burners to the required temperature according to your recipe.

2 Place the food on the cooking grate (see **figure 10**). Close the lid and cook directly over the heat source. The heat

figure 10

cooks the food from directly underneath (see **figure 11**). The food should be turned once halfway through the cooking time.

figure 11

Indirect cooking

This method is recommended for roasts, ribs, whole poultry and other large cuts of meat which take longer than 25 minutes. For best results always cook with the lid on.

1 Ignite the grill, and turn all burners onto High, close lid and leave to come up to heat.

2 Place the food in the centre of the cooking grate and turn off the burner(s) directly below the food. Adjust the burners on either side of the food to

the temperature according to the recipe. Close the lid and cook indirectly (see **figure 12**). The heat rises around the food and reflects off the inside

figure 12

surfaces of the grill cooking the food evenly on all sides. This circulating heat works like a convection oven, so there's no need to turn the food (see **figure 13**).

figure 13

Helpful grilling tips & hints

Cooking guidelines

■ Different foods require different cooking methods. It is important to understand the difference between the Direct and Indirect cooking methods.

■ Don't try to shave off time by placing food on a grill that's not quite ready, particularly a charcoal grill. Let charcoal burn until it has a light grey-ash coating (keep the vents open

so the fire doesn't go out). Make sure your gas grill has reached a temperature of at least 500°F/260°C before starting to cook.

■ You will control flare-ups, reduce cooking time, and get altogether better results if you grill with the lid down.

■ Unless the recipe calls for it, only turn your food once half-way through the cooking time.

■ Cooking times are affected by such factors as altitude, wind, outside temperature and desired doneness.

■ A crowded cooking grate of food will require a little more cooking time. Make sure that individual pieces of food do not touch allowing the heat to cook all sides.

■ Trim excess fat from steaks, chops and roasts leaving no more than a 5mm/$^1/_4$-inch thick layer. This helps avoid flare-ups.

■ A light coating of oil will help brown your food evenly and keep it from sticking to the cooking grate. Always brush or spray oil on your food, not the cooking grate.

■ When using a marinade, glaze or sauce with high sugar content, or any other ingredient that burns easily, only brush on the food during the last 10–15 minutes of cooking.

■ Spatulas or tongs are best for turning food on the grill. Avoid using a fork as this can cause juices and flavour to escape. Resist the urge to use your spatula to press down on foods such as burgers. You'll squeeze out all of that wonderful flavour.

Safety guidelines

■ Always follow the specific instructions in your owner's manual on safely lighting and operating your grill.

■ Stand the barbecue on a firm, level surface at least 2 feet away from buildings and anything else that could catch fire, such as fences and trees.

■ Never use a grill indoors (that includes your garage) or under a covered patio.

■ If using a commercially-prepared lighter fluid (never use petrol or highly volatile fluids), allow it to soak into the charcoal before igniting.

■ Never add lighter fluid to a lit fire.

■ Keep children and pets away from the heat source and potentially hot utensils.

■ Always use long-handled tools and long mitts to keep your hand and arm safe from the heat of the grill.

■ Never pour water on a grease fire. Instead, cover charcoal grills and close all vents; turn off gas grills at the source.

■ When you're finished using your charcoal grill, close the lid and all the vents. Check that hot coals are fully extinguished before leaving the barbecue.

■ Do not store a propane tank in an enclosed space including your house, garage or shed.

■ After using your gas grill, turn off the burners and then turn off the gas supply at the source.

Food safety

■ Wash your hands thoroughly with soap and warm water before starting any meal preparation and after handling fresh meat, fish or poultry.

■ Defrost meat, fish and poultry only in the refrigerator, never at room temperature.

■ If a sauce will be brushed on meat during grilling, divide the sauce, using one part for brushing and the other for serving at the table. Vigorously boil marinades that were used for raw meats, fish or poultry for 1 full minute before using as a baste or sauce.

■ Remember to always use separate utensils, chopping boards and plates for raw and cooked foods.

■ Always grill ground meats to at least 160°F/71°C (170°F/77°C for poultry).

■ Be sure to chill any leftover cooked food from the grill once it has cooked.

Accessories

While there's no need to buy every gadget ever invented for outdoor cooking, there are a few essentials that will make the job easier and, more importantly, safer. A general rule of thumb is to choose long-handled tools.

▲ **Long-handled equipment not only makes the job safer but also quicker and more efficient.**

■ An extra wide metal **spatula** is best for turning burgers, steaks and delicate fish fillets. A good, sturdy stainless steel blade is best.

■ A brass bristle **grill brush** makes cleaning the cooking grate easier. When the grill is hot, brush off food residue. Brass is rust resistant, so it's best for outdoors.

■ A pair of **spring-hinged tongs** is great for lifting and turning most types of food. Choose one with stainless steel ends and long handles.

■ A **long-handled fork** helps lift cooked roasts and whole poultry from the grill. Avoid piercing food while it's cooking because valuable juices will be lost. Also avoid using a fork on smaller cuts of meat.

■ A **vegetable wok/grill topper** makes grilling small and very delicate vegetables easy.

■ A **basting brush** is a must for brushing the food lightly with oil before cooking, to prevent food from sticking. This can also be used to brush food during cooking. Choose one with natural bristles.

■ **Skewers** are an excellent way of cooking meats or fish with vegetables all at the same time. It's also a much quicker and easier way to rotate a few kebabs than spending time turning over individual meats or fish and a variety of vegetables. Skewers are available in various lengths and are made from all kinds of different materials. Metal skewers are the most common, are good conductors of heat and are reusable. Double prong skewers prevent food from turning on the skewer. Disposable wooden or bamboo skewers are also good but they must be soaked in cold water for at least 30 minutes before you use them.

■ A **timer** is not essential but is a very useful accessory for one reason in particular: cooking under a lid puts the food out of sight and sometimes out of mind, especially if you are nipping in and out to the kitchen. The timer can be useful to remind you when food needs to be turned, checked or taken off the grill.

■ A **meat thermometer** is a great aid for cooking as it helps you to achieve perfectly cooked roast meat every time.

The thermometer indicates the internal temperature of the meat being cooked. It should be inserted into the centre of the thickest part of the meat when you think the meat is cooked. Wait a few minutes and you can check the thermometer against the temperature on the cooking charts (see charts for poultry on page 39 and meat on page 57). Do not leave the thermometer in the meat during cooking.

■ A good quality **oven glove** provides protection from pans or utensils and the grill itself. A gauntlet style glove also helps protect the cook's forearm.

Cleaning your grill

The easiest way to keep your grill clean is to heat it up and clean it before cooking, each time. When the barbecue is hot, use a long-handled grill brush or crumpled aluminium foil to rub the loosened particles from the cooking grates. The heat virtually 'sterilises' the cooking grates, and brushing them eliminates any remnant flavours, fats or food particles. This cleaning tip applies equally to charcoal grills.

◄ **A long-handled brush is vital for cleaning the cooking grate each time you use your grill.**

Marinades

Marinades enhance the flavour of meats, fish or vegetables. Cheaper cuts of meat benefit from a soaking in olive oil and a mixture of favourite herbs or spices. Most marinades use an oil base which helps keep the meat or fish moist during cooking. To avoid flare-ups, brush off any excess before placing the food on the grill.

Meat, fish or poultry should always be left to marinate in the refrigerator. While marinated fish and poultry should be transferred directly from the refrigerator to the barbecue, meat (with the exception of ground beef), should be brought to room temperature 20 to 30 minutes before barbecuing. Keep meat or fish covered during marinating and turn the pieces halfway through, to ensure the food has been covered equally. Do not use leftover marinade on the finished dish, as it has been in contact with raw meat. As a general guide marinate meat and chicken for about an hour and fish for about 30 minutes. Slashes or cuts applied to the meat or fish will help the flavours to penetrate and speed up the process.

The following recipes are for about 900g/ 2lb of meat or fish.

Lemon, garlic & oregano marinade

Use for lamb, pork, veal, chicken, turkey or fish.

150ml/$^{1}/_{4}$ pint olive oil
1 lemon, juice and pared rind
1 large garlic clove, thinly sliced
2 tablespoons fresh oregano, roughly torn
salt and freshly ground black pepper

Mix all the ingredients well in a bowl. Arrange the raw food in a shallow dish and pour over the marinade. Cover and marinate meat or poultry for 1 hour, fish for 30 minutes in the refrigerator.

Spiced ginger & yoghurt marinade

For lamb, chicken, duck, turkey or fish.

225g/8oz natural yoghurt
2 garlic cloves, crushed
2.5cm/1 inch piece of fresh ginger, grated
½ lemon, juice only
1 teaspoon ground cumin
1 teaspoon ground coriander
½ teaspoon crushed cardamom
½ teaspoon cayenne pepper
½ teaspoon salt
3 tablespoons fresh mint, roughly torn

Pour the yoghurt into a bowl. Add all the other ingredients and stir together well. Arrange the meat, chicken or fish in a shallow dish and pour over the marinade. Cover and marinate the meat or chicken in the refrigerator for 1 hour, fish for 30 minutes, turning once.

Classic Chinese marinade

For beef, pork, chicken, duck or fish.

2 tablespoons rice wine vinegar
4 tablespoons soy sauce
1 tablespoon sesame oil
2 tablespoons liquid honey
2.5cm/1 inch piece fresh root ginger, grated
2 garlic cloves, roughly chopped
1 teaspoon five spice powder

Whisk the ingredients together in a bowl. Arrange the raw food in a single layer in a shallow dish and pour over the marinade. Cover and marinate meat or poultry in the refrigerator for 1 hour, fish for 30 minutes.

Herb & spice rubs

Think of a 'rub' as a drier version of a marinade. While most marinades are oil based and work by seeping flavour into meat or fish, the rub is, as the name implies, literally rubbed into the food before it's cooked. A splash of oil can be added to rubs to make them more paste like if you prefer. Make shallow cuts in the food before applying the rub. Cover and refrigerate for about an hour before grilling to give the best results. If you are short on time rubs have the advantage of being quicker than marinades as the food absorbs the flavours instantly and can be cooked straight away with good results.

As most spice rubs are made with dry ingredients and are quick to put together, there is little point in making them in advance, but any left over will keep for several weeks stored in a sealed jar in a cool dry cupboard. The great joy in making spice and herb rubs is the endless combinations you can create. The following recipes will give you a good guideline as to the general quantities you will require, but after that, the larder or garden is your limit.

The following recipes yield enough mixture for about 900g/2lb of meat, poultry or fish.

Lemon herb rub

For pork, chicken, turkey or fish.

4 large garlic cloves, crushed
1 lemon, grated rind only
2 teaspoons dried rosemary, chopped
1 teaspoon dried basil leaves, chopped
½ teaspoon salt
½ teaspoon dried thyme leaves, chopped
½ teaspoon freshly ground black pepper

Put all the ingredients into a bowl and mix well.

Texas dry rub

For lamb, pork, veal, chicken or turkey.

1 garlic clove, crushed
1 teaspoon mustard seeds, crushed
1 tablespoon salt
1 teaspoon chilli powder
1 teaspoon cayenne pepper
1 teaspoon paprika
½ teaspoon ground coriander
½ teaspoon ground cumin

Put the garlic and mustard seeds into a mortar and pestle and grind to a paste. Add the remaining ingredients to the bowl and mix together well to form a dry rub.

Moroccan spice rub

For lamb, chicken, duck, turkey or fish.

1 teaspoon ground cumin
1 lemon, finely grated rind only
½ teaspoon saffron powder
1 teaspoon hot chilli powder
½ teaspoon ground coriander
2 tablespoons fresh coriander, finely chopped
1 garlic clove, finely chopped
¼ teaspoon sea salt
½ teaspoon freshly ground black pepper

Put all the ingredients into a mortar and pestle and rub or mix together thoroughly into a paste.

Flavoured butters

Flavoured butters make brilliant instant 'sauces' for grilled meats, chicken or fish. A simple barbecued steak, chicken or fish fillet from the grill turns into a flavourful meal with the addition of your favourite butter. You can prepare them in advance and there are many flavours you can create by simply stirring together your choice of herbs, spices or flavourings into softened butter. Spoon the butter onto a large sheet of greaseproof paper, rolling up the butter inside the paper into a log shape, and secure the ends like a Christmas cracker. Chill in the fridge to firm up. To serve, simply cut the log into thick slices and put a slice on the hot meat or fish as soon as it comes off the grill. Flavoured butters can be frozen to keep longer.

Provençal herb butter
For chicken, pork, lamb, fish and shellfish.

1 teaspoon fresh thyme, chopped
1 teaspoon fresh marjoram, chopped
1 teaspoon fresh basil, chopped
1 teaspoon fresh oregano, chopped
225g/8oz butter, softened

Beat the fresh herbs into the butter, roll up and chill until firm.

Lemon & fennel butter
For chicken, pork, fish and shellfish.

1 teaspoon fennel seeds
225g/8oz butter, softened
1 lemon, grated rind only
1 tablespoon fresh fennel, chopped

Dry fry the fennel seeds in a small frying pan for 1 minute until they smell aromatic. Put into a mortar and pestle and roughly grind. Stir into the softened butter with the lemon rind and fresh fennel, roll up and chill until firm.

Three pepper butter

For beef, pork and fish.

225g/8oz butter, softened
1 teaspoon pink peppercorns in brine, drained
1 teaspoon green peppercorns in brine, drained
1 teaspoon freshly ground black peppercorns

Beat all the ingredients together, roll up and chill until firm.

Coriander & orange butter

For beef, pork and fish.

225g/8oz butter, softened
1 orange, grated rind only
2 tablespoons fresh coriander, chopped

Beat all the ingredients together, roll up and chill until firm.

Roasted chilli butter

For beef, pork, vegetables and fish.

5 large red chillies
1 tablespoon olive oil
2 tablespoons fresh parsley, chopped
225g/8oz butter, softened

Put the chillies into a small roasting tray and brush with the oil. Roast in the oven at 230°C/450°F/Gas 8 for 10–15 minutes. Cool and scrape out the seeds then roughly chop the chillies. Beat into the butter with the parsley, roll up and chill until firm.

Fish & shellfish

Nothing captures the true spirit of outdoor cooking as much as the sizzling aroma of fresh fish or shellfish. Some outdoor cooks see fish as difficult and time consuming when in fact the opposite is true. Small whole fish and shellfish are a gift to the barbecue, with little preparation needed before grilling.

When choosing fish for the barbecue it is important to remember to select fish suitable for grilling and to choose the freshest fish available. Fresh fish should have a wonderful aroma of the sea and not a strong 'fishy' smell, and the eyes should be bright and clear. Lift up the gill cover and check the gills, which should be bright pink (not dull or red). The scales should be shiny and tight around the fish. If you are grilling fish whole it will need to be gutted and the scales and fins removed. (Whether to grill with the head on or off is up to you.)

Safety points

- Fish and shellfish should always have a pleasant smell of the sea and not a strong fishy smell.
- Keep all fresh fish well refrigerated. It's best to grill fish on the day of purchase.
- Wash fish well before preparing and grilling.
- When preparing mussels, clams and scallops ensure they are all tightly closed. Any that are open should be tapped sharply with the back of a knife and, if they do not close, should be discarded immediately. Similarly, discard any that have not opened after cooking.
- Thoroughly wash your hands, utensils, chopping boards and work surfaces after preparing raw fish and shellfish. Raw fish is not necessarily unsafe but it can contaminate the flavours of other foods easily.

To check when a fillet is cooked cut it open to see (usually at the point when the centre is changing from translucent to opaque). With experience you will know whether it is done just by touch, the flesh will be firm and will give slightly when ready. Shellfish only take a few minutes on the grill; wherever possible, grill them with the shells on to retain their juices.

Type of fish & shellfish	Thickness or weight	Cooking time/method
fish fillet or steak	1.5cm/$\frac{1}{2}$ inch thick	3–5 mins / DH
	2cm/$\frac{3}{4}$ inch thick	5–10 mins / DH
	2.5cm/1 inch thick	10–12 mins / DH
fish kebab	2.5cm/1 inch thick	8–10 mins / DM
fish, whole	450g/1lb (5–6.5cm/2–2$\frac{1}{2}$ inches thick)	15–20 mins / IM
	450–900g/1–2lb	20–30 mins / IM
	900g–1.75kg/2–4lb	30–45 mins / IM
crab	approx. 1.2kg/2$\frac{1}{2}$lb	10–12 mins / DM
lobster, split lengthwise	approx. 900g/2lb	8–10 mins / DM
lobster tail	225–300g/8–10oz	8–12 mins / DM
prawn with shell	medium	4–5 mins / DH
	large	5–6 mins / DH
	extra large	6–8 mins / DH
prawn without shell	about 1–2 mins less than the above timings / DH	
scallop without shell	2.5–5cm/1–2 inches diameter	3–6 mins / DH
clam	medium	8–10 mins / DH (discard any that do not open)
oyster	small	3–6 mins / DH
mussel	medium	5–6 mins / DH (discard any that do not open)

Grilled oysters in buttery barbecue sauce

12 fresh oysters

Barbecue sauce

1 tablespoon unsalted butter

1 teaspoon minced garlic

2 tablespoons freshly squeezed lemon juice

2 tablespoons mild chilli sauce

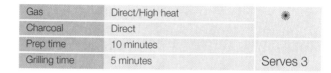

Gas	Direct/High heat	✳
Charcoal	Direct	
Prep time	10 minutes	
Grilling time	5 minutes	Serves 3

1 To make the **barbecue sauce**: Sauté the butter and garlic in a saucepan over medium heat, stirring occasionally until the garlic aroma is apparent and the butter begins to brown, about 2–3 minutes. Remove the garlic butter from the heat and add the lemon juice and chilli sauce. Mix until well blended.

2 To open the **oysters**: Grip each oyster flat side up in a folded kitchen towel. Find a small opening between the shells near the hinge and prise open with an oyster knife. Try to keep the juices in the shell. Loosen the oyster from the shell by running the oyster knife carefully underneath the body. Discard the top, flatter shell, keeping the oyster in the bottom, deeper shell.

3 Spoon ½ teaspoon of barbecue sauce over each oyster. Barbecue the oysters over Direct High heat, until the sauce boils inside the shell, after 2–3 minutes, then barbecue oysters for 1–2 minutes more. Serve warm.

Salt-crusted prawns with herb dipping sauce

Herb dipping sauce

120ml/4 fl oz extra virgin olive oil
1 lemon, juice only
50ml/2fl oz boiling water
2 garlic cloves, crushed
1 teaspoon dried oregano
2 tablespoons fresh parsley, chopped

Salt-crusted prawns

500g/1¼lb large whole raw prawns
3 tablespoons olive oil
65g/2½oz sea salt

Gas	Direct/Medium heat	☀
Charcoal	Direct	
Prep time	25 minutes	
Grilling time	6–8 minutes	Serves 4

1 To make the **herb dipping sauce**: Whisk together the extra virgin olive oil, lemon juice and hot water. Stir in the garlic, oregano and parsley. Set aside for 20 minutes for the flavours to develop.

2 Meanwhile, prepare the **salt-crusted prawns**. Use a small knife to make a slit down the backs of the prawns and remove the vein, but do not remove the shells.

3 Put the prawns in a large bowl and toss with the olive oil to coat. Add the salt and mix well, ensuring that each prawn gets a good coating of salt. Thread 2 or 3 prawns at a time onto wooden skewers, to help turn them while they are grilling.

4 Barbecue the salt-crusted prawns over Direct Medium heat for 6–8 minutes, turning once, until tender. Serve warm with the herb dipping sauce.

Tiger prawns with hot sweet sauce

16 tiger prawns, peeled and
   deveined
1 garlic clove, finely
   chopped
2 tablespoons olive oil
salt and freshly ground
   black pepper

Hot sweet sauce
1 garlic clove, crushed
2 tablespoons light soy
   sauce
3 tablespoons liquid honey
1 lime, grated rind and juice
2 tablespoons fresh
   coriander, roughly
   chopped
1 teaspoon chilli flakes

Gas	Direct/Medium heat	☀ ☀
Charcoal	Direct	
Prep time	25 minutes + 25 mins marinating	
Grilling time	2–3 minutes	Serves 4

1 Cut 8 bamboo skewers to 10cm/4 inches in length. Soak in cold water for at least 30 minutes. Rinse prawns and pat dry on kitchen paper. Put into a bowl with the chopped garlic and olive oil. Season well and toss. Cover and leave to marinate in the refrigerator for 15 minutes.

2 To make the **hot sweet sauce**: Put the crushed garlic, soy sauce, honey, grated rind of the whole lime and the juice of half the lime, coriander and chilli flakes in a bowl. Whisk together until the honey has dissolved into the other ingredients. Put into a small dish for dipping.

3 Thread two prawns onto each skewer. Barbecue over Direct Medium heat for 2–3 minutes, turning once halfway through grilling time, until pink and tender. Serve warm with the sauce.

Crab fishcakes with chilli dipping sauce

175g/6oz firm white fish,
such as cod, hake or
haddock
250g/9oz fresh or canned
white crab meat
125g/4oz can sweetcorn,
drained
1 red chilli, deseeded and
chopped
2 spring onions, finely
chopped
2 tablespoons fresh
coriander, chopped
1 tablespoon Thai fish
sauce
1 egg, beaten
salt and freshly ground
black pepper
oil, for brushing

Chilli dipping sauce
6 tablespoons rice wine
vinegar
1 teaspoon caster sugar
1 birds eye chilli, sliced

Gas	Direct/Medium heat	✳ ✳
Charcoal	Direct	
Prep time	30 minutes + 1 hour chilling	
Grilling time	7–8 minutes	Serves 6

1 Remove any skin and bones from the white fish. Cut the flesh into pieces and put into a food processor and blend for a few seconds until a paste is formed. Scrape out and put into a bowl. Stir in the crab meat.

2 Add to the sweetcorn, chilli, spring onion, coriander, fish sauce, egg and seasoning. Mix together very well until all the ingredients are well combined.

3 Divide the mixture into twelve parts and shape each into a round cake about 2cm/¾ inch thick. Put on a tray and chill for at least 1 hour to firm up.

4 Meanwhile, to make the **chilli dipping sauce**: Mix the rice wine vinegar, caster sugar and chilli together. Put aside.

5 Brush the cakes with oil and barbecue over Direct Medium heat for 7–8 minutes turning once halfway through cooking time, until browned. Serve with the chilli dipping sauce.

4 salmon fillets or salmon
   steaks, about 225g/8oz
   each in weight
1 garlic clove, crushed
1 lemon grass stem, chopped
2 red chillies, deseeded and
   sliced
1 lime, juice only
2 tablespoons Thai fish sauce
4 tablespoons sunflower oil

Pad Thai noodles

225g/8oz sen lek Thai
   noodles (flat flour noodles)
2 tablespoons peanut oil
2 tablespoons sunflower oil
1 garlic clove, chopped
1 shallot, chopped
1 red chilli, deseeded and
   finely shredded
2 tablespoons Thai fish sauce
1 lime, juice only
1 teaspoon brown sugar
small bunch spring onions,
   finely shredded
50g/2oz roasted peanuts,
   roughly chopped
50g/2oz bean sprouts
2 tablespoons fresh
   coriander, chopped

Thai salmon with noodles

Gas	Direct/Medium heat	✳ ✳ ✳
Charcoal	Direct	
Prep time	25 minutes + 30 mins marinating	
Grilling time	6–8 minutes	Serves 4

1 Put the salmon into a large shallow dish in a single layer. In a small bowl mix the crushed garlic, lemon grass, sliced chillies, lime juice, Thai fish sauce and sunflower oil. Pour over the salmon and leave to marinate, covered, in the refrigerator for 30 minutes.

2 Meanwhile, to make the **Pad Thai noodles**: Cook the noodles in boiling salted water according to the packet instructions until tender. Drain and refresh under cold running water. Drain again. Heat the peanut and sunflower oils in a wok, add the chopped garlic and shallot and fry for 1–2 minutes until just golden. Add the chilli, fish sauce, lime juice and sugar, cooking for 30 seconds, and remove from heat. Toss with the noodles, half the spring onions, bean sprouts and peanuts. Put aside.

3 Scrape excess marinade off the salmon steaks and barbecue them over Direct Medium heat for 6–8 minutes, turning once halfway through grilling time.

4 Sprinkle the coriander and the remaining spring onions over the Pad Thai noodles. Serve with the hot salmon steaks.

Teriyaki fish steaks with green & black rice

3 tablespoons sake
  (Japanese rice wine)
3 tablespoons dry sherry
3 tablespoons dark soy
  sauce
1½ tablespoons soft brown
  sugar
4 fish steaks, about
  175–200g/6–7oz each
  in weight

Green & black rice
salt
350g/12oz long-grain and
  wild rice
2.5cm/1 inch piece of fresh
  ginger
225g/8oz mange tout
small bunch spring onions,
  cut into fine strips

Gas	Direct/Medium heat	❋ ❋ ❋
Charcoal	Direct	
Prep time	25 minutes + 30 mins marinating	
Grilling time	6 minutes	Serves 4

1 Put the sake, sherry, soy sauce and brown sugar into a small saucepan and heat until the sugar dissolves, then bring to the boil and remove from the heat. Leave to cool.

2 Put the fish steaks into a shallow dish in a single layer and pour over the cold teriyaki sauce. Leave to marinate, covered, for 30 minutes in the refrigerator, turning once.

3 Meanwhile, to make the **green and black rice**: Bring a large pan of salted water to the boil and add the piece of ginger and the long grain and wild rice. Cook according to packet instruction until just tender. Cut each mange tout lengthways into 3 or 4 strips and cook in boiling salted water for 2 minutes. Drain and refresh under cold running water. Drain the rice, remove the ginger and discard. Stir the mange tout and spring onions into the hot rice.

4 Remove the steaks from the marinade and barbecue over Direct Medium heat for 5–6 minutes, turning once and brushing a few times with the reserved teriyaki sauce. Serve with the hot green and black rice.

Grilled mackerel with tangy dill dressing

4 gutted mackerel
a small bunch fresh dill
oil, for brushing

Dill dressing
1 lemon
2 tablespoons olive oil
1 small onion, chopped
1 garlic clove, crushed
200g/7oz can chopped
  tomatoes
4 tablespoons red wine
  vinegar
1 teaspoon caster sugar
120ml/4fl oz extra virgin
  olive oil
2 tablespoons fresh chives,
  chopped
2 tablespoons capers,
  drained
salt and freshly ground
  black pepper

Gas	Direct/Medium heat	❊ ❊ ❊
Charcoal	Direct	
Prep time	40 minutes	
Grilling time	12 minutes	Serves 4

1 Wash the mackerel under cold running water and cut off the fins. Make three or four deep slashes through to the bone in each side of the mackerel. Stuff each slash with a small sprig of dill and leave aside. Chop remaining dill and reserve.

2 To make the **dill dressing**: Heat the olive oil in a small saucepan and cook the onion and garlic for 2–3 minutes until softened. Add the chopped tomatoes and simmer for 10–15 minutes. Meanwhile in a small clean saucepan put 2 tablespoons vinegar and the sugar and boil rapidly until reduced to about 2 teaspoonfuls. Combine with the tomato mixture and stir in well.

3 Press the tomato mixture through a sieve and return to a clean saucepan and cook for 1–2 minutes until thickened. Leave the mixture to cool.

4 Put 2 tablespoons vinegar into a bowl with the olive oil, the chopped dill, chives, and seasoning and whisk well. Stir the tomato mixture and capers into the herb vinaigrette.

5 Brush the mackerel with a little oil. Barbecue over Direct Medium heat for 10–12 minutes until tender, turning once halfway through cooking time. Serve hot with the cool dressing.

Aussie prawn & scallop skewers

175g/6oz mango chutney
120ml/4fl oz orange juice
115g/4oz sweet and tangy
    barbecue sauce
8 baby onions or shallots
8 fresh pineapple chunks,
    about 2.5cm/1 inch
12 large raw prawns, peeled
    and deveined
12 large scallops
8 cherry tomatoes
salt and pepper

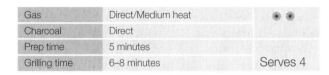

Gas	Direct/Medium heat	☀ ☀
Charcoal	Direct	
Prep time	5 minutes	
Grilling time	6–8 minutes	Serves 4

1 Soak four bamboo skewers in cold water for 30 minutes. Put the mango chutney, orange juice and barbecue sauce into a food processor or blender and blend until smooth. Set aside.

2 Put the onions or shallots into a small saucepan and cover with water. Bring to the boil and simmer for 1 minute then drain and refresh immediately under cold running water. When cool enough to handle, peel and set aside.

3 Thread the pineapple, prawns, scallops, tomatoes and onion (or shallots) onto the skewers. Season and brush liberally with the reserved sauce. Barbecue over Direct Medium heat for 6–8 minutes, or until the prawns and scallops are tender, turning once and brushing with sauce. Serve with remaining sauce for dipping.

Salmon fillets with basil & mint crème

25g/1oz fresh basil leaves

25g/1oz fresh mint leaves

200ml/7fl oz light olive oil

1 egg yolk

1 teaspoon Dijon mustard

salt and freshly ground
black pepper

1 lime, finely grated rind
and juice

2 tablespoons crème
fraiche

4 salmon fillets with skin
on, each weighing
about 225g/8oz

oil, for brushing

Gas	Direct/Medium heat	✹ ✹
Charcoal	Direct	
Prep time	30 minutes	
Grilling time	8 minutes	Serves 4

1 Bring a pan of water to the boil and add the basil and mint leaves for 15 seconds. Remove the herbs and drain well; absorb excess water on kitchen paper. Put into a food processor with the olive oil and blend well. Leave aside for 15 minutes to infuse.

2 Put the egg yolk, mustard and plenty of seasoning into a bowl and whisk until smooth. Gradually blend in the basil and mint olive oil a trickle at a time until all the oil is added and the mixture is thick and smooth. Whisk in the lime juice and rind, stir in the crème fraiche, then chill.

3 Brush the salmon fillets with oil and barbecue skin side down over Direct Medium heat for 4 minutes. Brush with a little more oil, then turn over and cook for a further 4 minutes. Serve hot with the basil and mint crème.

Poultry

A plump, juicy chicken, turkey or duck with seared crispy skin is the hero of the barbecue. These versatile meats are suitable for a host of diverse recipes – make it spicy with hot flavours from Mexico and India, or try the sweet and sour tastes of China and Thailand. And to enjoy ingredients closer to home, try soft-scented herbs or the zing of lemon and lime.

When it comes to poultry, we are spoiled for choice. There are handy-packed portions or whole oven-ready birds ranging from corn-fed, free range or organic. If you intend to marinate with strong flavours or spices you can safely choose a cheaper breed or cut. Less aromatic treatments or simple plain grilling call for a better quality bird. Chicken tastes best when grilled with its skin still on. It can of course be grilled without the skin but, because most of the fat lies just underneath, removing it will mean that the chicken will need extra oil or marinade to keep it moist. Always wash the meat under cold running water and pat dry on kitchen paper before preparing.

Safety points

- Always keep raw or cooked poultry refrigerated when not using, keeping them well separated.
- Always thaw chicken in the refrigerator.
- Thoroughly wash your hands, utensils, chopping boards and work surfaces after preparing raw poultry.
- Never use the same chopping boards, utensils or dishes for raw and cooked poultry.
- Always cook chicken well. To test if it's cooked through, use a food thermometer to check the internal temperature, or insert a knife into the thickest part of the piece such as the thigh. Juices should run clear with no traces of blood.

Type of poultry	Thickness or weight	Cooking time/method	Internal temp.
chicken, whole	1.5–2.25kg/3$\frac{1}{2}$–5lb	1–1$\frac{1}{2}$ hours / IM	180F/82C
chicken half (bone-in)	675–800g/1$\frac{1}{4}$–1$\frac{1}{2}$lb	1–1$\frac{1}{4}$ hours / IM	180F/82C
chicken breast (boneless, skinless)	175g/6oz	8–12 mins / DM	170F/77C
chicken pieces, breast or wing (bone-in)	approx.225g/8oz	30–40 mins / IM	180F/82C
chicken pieces, leg or thigh (bone-in)	100–175g/4–6oz	40–50 mins / IM	180F/82C
chicken thigh (boneless, skinless)	100g/4oz	8–10 mins / DM	180F/82C
chicken kebab	2.5cm/1 inch dice	6–8 mins / DM	180F/77C
chicken burger	2cm/$\frac{3}{4}$ inch thick	10–12 mins / DM	170F/77C
poussin, whole	350g–450g/12oz–1lb	40–50 mins / IM	180F/82C
turkey, whole (unstuffed)	4.5–5kg/10–11lb	1$\frac{3}{4}$–2$\frac{1}{2}$ hours / IM	180F/82C
	5.5–6.5kg/12–14lb	2$\frac{1}{4}$–3 hours / IM	180F/82C
	6.75–7.5kg/15–17lb	2$\frac{3}{4}$–3$\frac{3}{4}$ hours / IM	
	8–10kg/18–22lb	3$\frac{1}{2}$–4 hours / IM	180F/82C
	(general guideline: 11–13 mins per 450g/lb)		
turkey breast (bone-in)	1.5 kg/4–5lb	1–1$\frac{1}{2}$ hours / IM	170F/82C
turkey drumstick (bone-in)	450–675g/$\frac{1}{2}$–1$\frac{1}{2}$lb	$\frac{3}{4}$–1$\frac{1}{4}$ hours / IM	180F/82C
turkey breast escalope	5mm–1cm/$\frac{1}{4}$–$\frac{1}{2}$ inch thick	4–6 mins / DM	170F/77C
turkey breast (boneless)	1.75kg/4lb	1 hour / DM	170F/77C
duck, whole	1.75–2.75kg/4–6lb	1$\frac{1}{2}$–2 hours / IM	180F/82C
duck breast (boneless)	250–300g/9–10oz (approx.1.5cm–$\frac{1}{2}$ inch thick)	12–14 mins / DL	180F/82C
goose, whole	4.5–6.5kg/10–12lb	3 hours / IM	180F/82C

Chicken fajita skewers with guacamole salsa

3 tablespoons olive oil

1 garlic clove, crushed

½ teaspoon ground cumin

½ teaspoon ground
coriander

1 teaspoon chilli powder

salt and freshly ground
black pepper

4 boneless, skinless
chicken breasts

1 red pepper

1 green pepper

1 onion

Guacamole salsa

2 ripe, but firm avocados

1 lime, juice only

1 large red chilli, deseeded
and finely chopped

6 spring onions, finely
chopped

3 tomatoes, peeled,
deseeded and diced

3 tablespoons fresh
coriander, chopped

Gas	Direct/Medium heat	✳ ✳
Charcoal	Direct	
Prep time	35 minutes + 30 mins marinating	
Grilling time	10–12 minutes	Serves 4

1 Put the olive oil, garlic, cumin, ground coriander, chilli powder and seasoning into a bowl and mix well. Cut the chicken into bite size pieces and add to the marinade. Mix well and leave for 30 minutes in the refrigerator. Meanwhile soak eight bamboo skewers in cold water for 30 minutes.

2 Halve and deseed the peppers. Cut each half into even bite size pieces and put aside. Cut the onion into eight wedges and leave aside.

3 Alternately thread pieces of chicken, red and green pepper and onion wedges onto the skewers. Brush any marinade remaining in the bowl onto the peppers and onion pieces.

4 Barbecue over Direct Medium heat for 10–12 minutes, until tender.

5 Meanwhile, to make the **guacamole salsa**: Halve, stone and peel the avocados. Cut the flesh into neat dice, put into a bowl and add the rest of the guacamole ingredients, tossing well so that the avocado is coated in the lime juice.

6 Serve the hot skewers with guacamole salsa.

Spicy chicken pieces Tandoori-style

500g/1½ pints natural
  yoghurt
2.5cm/1 inch piece of fresh
  ginger, grated
3 garlic cloves, crushed
2 teaspoons paprika
2 teaspoons salt
1½ teaspoons ground
  cinnamon
1 teaspoon ground cumin
1 teaspoon ground
  coriander
freshly ground black pepper,
  to taste
¼ teaspoon ground cloves
1.5kg/3–3½lb chicken
  pieces with skin on
oil, for brushing
wedges of lime, to serve

Gas	Indirect/Medium heat
Charcoal	Indirect
Prep time	15 minutes + 8 hours marinating
Grilling time	1 hour 10 minutes

Serves 6

1 Put the yoghurt into a large bowl. Stir in the ginger, garlic, paprika, salt, cinnamon, cumin, coriander, pepper and cloves and mix well. Set aside.

2 Using a sharp knife, make two or three deep cuts in the chicken pieces. Add the chicken to the marinade and work the marinade into the cuts. Cover and leave to marinate in the refrigerator for at least 8 hours.

3 Scraping off most of the marinade from the chicken pieces, barbecue over Indirect Medium heat for 1 hour–1 hour and 10 minutes, turning once, until tender. Season and serve hot with wedges of lime and warm Naan bread.

Stuffed chicken legs with grilled red peppers

20g/¾oz fresh coriander
25g/1oz fresh basil
40g/1½oz Parmesan
  cheese, freshly grated
4 whole chicken legs
4 red peppers
salt and pepper

Gas	Indirect/Medium heat	☀
Charcoal	Indirect	
Prep time	15 minutes	
Grilling time	35–45 minutes	

Serves 4

1 Put the coriander, basil and Parmesan cheese into a food processor and blend until finely chopped.

2 Cut off any excess fat from the chicken legs. Work your fingers under the skin to loosen it from the flesh of the thigh and drumstick. Divide the coriander and basil mixture between the chicken legs and work it up under the skin, distributing the mixture evenly. Season the chicken well.

3 Put the chicken legs and the red peppers on the cooking grate and barbecue over Indirect Medium heat for 20 minutes turning the peppers once during cooking time.

4 Remove the peppers from the heat. Turn the chicken legs and continue cooking for a further 20–25 minutes until tender and the juices run clear.

5 Meanwhile, remove the skin, stems and seeds from the red peppers, reserving any juice that comes out of them. Remove the chicken from the grill and allow to rest for 5 minutes. Drizzle with the juice and serve warm with the grilled peppers.

Chicken burgers with blue cheese mayonnaise

500g/1¼lb boneless
  skinless chicken thighs,
  or 450g/1lb chopped
  chicken meat
6 rashers streaky bacon,
  rind removed
1 tablespoon olive oil
1 garlic clove, crushed
1 shallot, finely chopped
2 tablespoons fresh
  tarragon, roughly chopped
50g/2oz fresh white
  breadcrumbs

Blue cheese mayonnaise
1 egg yolk
1 teaspoon Dijon mustard
150ml/¼ pint light olive oil
1 teaspoon white wine
  vinegar
75g/3oz blue cheese
1 tablespoon fresh chives,
  chopped

4 burger buns

Gas	Direct/Medium heat	✳ ✳
Charcoal	Direct	
Prep time	30 minutes + chilling	
Grilling time	15 minutes	Serves 4

1 Cut the chicken thighs into pieces and put into a food processor. Cut two rashers of bacon into pieces and add to the chicken; blend until coarsely chopped. Heat the olive oil in a frying pan and add the garlic and shallot. Cook for 1–2 minutes until softened. Remove from pan, cool, and drain off excess oil.

2 Add the garlic and shallot and then the tarragon and bread-crumbs to the chicken mixture. Season and mix well. Divide into four parts. Lightly flour your hands to prevent mixture sticking then shape each part into a burger. Chill for 30 minutes.

3 To make the **blue cheese mayonnaise**: Whisk the egg yolk, mustard and plenty of seasoning in a bowl until smooth. Slowly whisk in the olive oil until the mixture is thick and smooth. Whisk in the vinegar. Crumble the blue cheese and fold into the mayonnaise. Add the chopped chives, and set aside to chill.

4 Grill the bacon for 8–10 minutes until crisp. Put aside. Brush the burgers with oil and barbecue them over Direct Medium heat for 15 minutes, turning once, until tender.

5 Toast the buns on the grill. Arrange salad leaves, a chicken burger, a spoonful of mayonnaise and a bacon rasher on one half of the bun and top with the other half.

Aromatic chicken with lemon balm or mint

1 lemon
50g/2oz caster sugar
1.5 kg/3–3½lb corn-fed
chicken
a bunch of lemon balm
or mint
1 teaspoon black
peppercorns
1 teaspoon coriander seeds
2 tablespoons olive oil
½ teaspoon salt

Gas	Indirect/Medium heat	✳ ✳
Charcoal	Indirect	
Prep time	20 minutes	
Grilling time	1¼ hours	Serves 4

1 Thinly slice the lemon. Bring a saucepan of water to the boil, add the lemon slices and cook for 2 minutes. Drain and refresh the blanched lemon slices under cold running water. Put the sugar and 150 ml/¼ pint water into a clean saucepan and bring to the boil. Add the blanched lemon slices and simmer for 10 minutes. Remove from heat and leave aside to cool.

2 Meanwhile, to prepare the chicken, work your fingers between the skin and the breast meat to loosen it and then loosen the skin on the legs. Drain the lemon slices. Work the lemon slices and lemon balm or mint up under the loosened skin, over the legs and breast meat.

3 Put the peppercorns and coriander seeds into a pestle and mortar and grind coarsely. Mix with the oil and brush all over the chicken. Place the chicken on the cooking grate and barbecue over Indirect Medium heat for 1–1¼ hours until the juices run clear and the internal temperature is 170°F/77°F. Leave the chicken to rest for 10–15 minutes before carving.

Spatchcocked poussin with apple glaze

4 poussins

8 bamboo skewers, soaked
  in cold water

Apple glaze

150ml/¼ pint pure apple
  juice

55g/2oz muscovado sugar

1 tablespoon cider vinegar

2 tablespoons tomato
  ketchup

1 orange, grated rind only

salt and freshly ground
  black pepper

Gas	Indirect/Medium heat
Charcoal	Indirect
Prep time	15 minutes
Grilling time	45 minutes

✴ ✴

Serves 4

1 Soak eight bamboo skewers in cold water for 30 minutes. Using poultry shears or large kitchen scissors cut along either side of the backbone on each poussin and remove the bone. Open out the birds and press down on the breastbone to flatten out. Pin each bird into shape by pushing a skewer through one leg to come out diagonally through the wing on the other side. Crisscross with a second skewer through the other leg and opposite wing. Repeat for all four birds.

2 To make the **apple glaze**: Put the apple juice, sugar and vinegar into a small saucepan, bring to the boil and reduce by half. Stir in the ketchup, orange rind and seasoning and mix well.

3 Put the poussins into a shallow dish and pour over the glaze. Brush well into each bird. Lift out poussins and let excess glaze run off.

4 Barbecue the poussins over Indirect Medium heat for 45–50 minutes. Brush quickly with remaining glaze every 15 minutes during grilling time. Poussins are done when juices run clear, and internal temperature in the thick part of the thigh reaches 170°F/77°C. Serve with salad.

Whole turkey stuffed with thyme & orange

1 teaspoon coriander seeds
225g/8oz butter, softened
2 large oranges
a large bunch thyme
4.5–5.5kg/10–12lb oven
   ready turkey
3 bay leaves
2 tablespoons olive oil
salt and freshly ground
   black pepper

Gas	Indirect/Medium heat	✳ ✳ ✳
Charcoal	Indirect	
Prep time	30 minutes	
Grilling time	2½–3 hours	Serves 10–12

1 Put the coriander seeds into a pestle and mortar and crush into a fine powder. Dry fry in a small frying pan for 1–2 minutes until it smells aromatic. Leave to cool.

2 Put the softened butter into a bowl and beat in the crushed roasted coriander. Grate the rind of the oranges and add to the butter, reserving the oranges. Add 2 tablespoons of fresh thyme leaves and beat the butter mixture until smooth. Put aside.

3 Starting at the neck end of the turkey, loosen the skin on the breast and legs, by easing your fingers between the meat and skin, taking care not to tear the skin. Ease the butter under the skin all over the breast and legs until all the butter is used up.

4 Halve the reserved oranges and put into the cavity with the bay leaves and stalks from the thyme leaves. Tie the legs together and brush the turkey with olive oil and season well.

5 Barbecue the stuffed turkey over Indirect Medium heat for 2½–3 hours (26 minutes per kg/11–13 minutes per lb) or until the juices run clear when skewered. The internal temperature in the meaty part of the thigh should be 170°F/77°C.

6 Transfer the turkey to a platter and then leave to stand for 20 minutes before carving.

Turkey escalopes with caramelised onions

6 tablespoons olive oil

2 red onions, finely sliced

1 teaspoon sugar

50 ml/2fl oz dry white wine

3½ tablespoons Dijon
  mustard

1 garlic clove, crushed

salt and freshly ground
  black pepper

2 tablespoons mayonnaise

4 turkey escalopes

1 ciabatta loaf

a handful of rocket leaves

Gas	Direct/Medium heat
Charcoal	Direct
Prep time	30 minutes
Grilling time	10 minutes

Serves 4

1 Heat 2 tablespoons of oil in a saucepan, add the sliced onions and sugar and cook very gently for 15 minutes until very soft and lightly golden. Add the white wine and bring to the boil until reduced. Put aside to cool.

2 In a small bowl mix the remaining 4 tablespoons of olive oil with 1½ tablespoons mustard and the crushed garlic clove and season well. Brush over the turkey escalopes and leave aside. Mix the remaining mustard with the mayonnaise and reserve.

3 Cut the ciabatta in half lengthways, then cut each half into two pieces and put them to the side.

4 Barbecue the turkey escalopes over Direct Medium heat for 4–5 minutes. Turn over and brush with the remaining mustard oil and cook for a further 2–3 minutes until tender.

5 Toast the ciabatta pieces on the grill, cut side down, for 1–2 minutes. Spread each piece of toasted ciabatta with mustard mayonnaise. Top with a turkey escalope. Spoon the caramelised onions on the escalopes and arrange a few rocket leaves on top.

Duck breasts with Indonesian marinade

4 boneless duck breasts
4 tablespoons soy sauce
2 tablespoons honey
1 tablespoon sesame seeds,
   toasted
3 garlic cloves, crushed
50ml/2fl oz chicken stock
1 teaspoon hoisin sauce
1½ teaspoons cornflour
1 tablespoon Sake
   (Japanese rice wine)
2 spring onions, finely
   chopped
rice or noodles, to serve

Gas	Direct/Low heat	✳ ✳
Charcoal	Direct	
Prep time	10 minutes + 24 hours marinating	
Grilling time	15 minutes	Serves 4

1 Using a sharp knife trim the skin of the duck breast to about 3mm/⅛ inch and cut off any excess fat or skin that overhangs the edge of the meat. Score the remaining fat in a diamond pattern, cutting the fat right through to the flesh. This helps the excess fat to drain away. Set aside.

2 Mix together the soy sauce, honey, sesame seeds and garlic to make a marinade. Put the duck into a large shallow dish in a single layer and pour over the marinade, turning the meat to coat. Cover and refrigerate for 24 hours turning occasionally.

3 Remove meat from marinade, reserving the marinade, and place in the centre of the cooking grate, skin side down. Barbecue over Direct Low heat for 10 minutes, turning once, then remove from the grill and leave to rest for 5 minutes.

4 Meanwhile, put the chicken stock, hoisin sauce and reserved marinade into a small saucepan, bring to the boil and simmer gently. In a small bowl, whisk together the cornflour and sake until smooth. Whisk into the saucepan and continue simmering until thickened (about 1–2 minutes).

5 Slice the duck breasts diagonally and spoon over the sauce. Sprinkle with the spring onions and serve with rice or noodles.

Orange duck breasts with red wine sauce

4 boneless duck breasts

1 large orange, grated rind
  and juice

1 garlic clove, crushed

1 shallot, finely chopped

1 bay leaf

240ml/8fl oz red wine

2 tablespoons balsamic
  vinegar

1 teaspoon sugar

salt and freshly ground
  black pepper

3 tablespoons redcurrant
  jelly

Gas	Direct/Low heat	✹ ✹
Charcoal	Direct	
Prep time	15 minutes + 1 hour marinating	
Grilling time	15 minutes	Serves 4

1 Using a sharp knife, cut off any excess fat or skin that overhangs the edge of the meat (see cook's note below). Score the fat in a diamond pattern cutting right through to the flesh. Put into a large shallow dish in a single layer and rub the grated orange rind into the scored fat. Scatter over the garlic and shallot, add a bay leaf and pour over orange juice and red wine. Leave to marinate in the refrigerator for at least 1 hour.

2 Remove the duck breasts from the marinade and drain well, pouring the remaining marinade into a small saucepan. Add the balsamic vinegar and sugar to the pan and bring to the boil, then simmer until reduced by half. Strain into a clean saucepan, season and whisk in the redcurrant jelly. Cook for a further 1–2 minutes until slightly thickened.

3 Meanwhile, put the duck breasts skin side down on the cooking grate and barbecue over Direct Low heat for 7–8 minutes until skin is golden brown. Turn over and cook for a further 6–7 minutes until they are just firm to the touch, for medium doneness (add another 3–4 minutes cooking time for well done). Slice the duck breasts and serve with the warm sauce.

Meat

Some of the best 'come and get it' aromas in the world are the rich, sweet, charred smells of meat grilling on a barbecue. Traditionally sausages, burgers and steaks have been the long-time favourites. Extending that repertoire to include joints such as rack of lamb, pork tenderloin and even whole glazed ham will result in an impressive range of tasty meals that are easy to cook on the barbecue.

When buying beef or lamb for grilling, look for meat with a good marbling of fat (tiny veins of fat running through the meat). Fat gives meat its flavour but as you will be trimming off most of the outer fat to avoid flare-ups, it is important to have good marbling.

Beef should have a bright red flesh while lamb has a dull red appearance. Pork and veal both have a pale pink flesh with no marbling. The fat of pork should be smooth and white while veal fat is pinkish white.

If possible buy your steaks from a butcher where you can ask for them to be cut to a certain thickness which will allow the grilling guides to be followed as closely as possible.

Safety points

- Always keep raw or cooked meat refrigerated when not using and never store them near each other.
- Always thaw meat in the refrigerator.
- Thoroughly wash your hands, utensils, chopping boards and work surfaces after preparing raw meat.
- Never use the same chopping boards, utensils or dishes for raw and cooked meat dishes.

Type of beef & veal	Thickness or weight	Cooking time/method	Internal temp.
steak: sirloin, T-bone or rib	2.5cm/1 inch thick	10–12 mins / DM	160F/71C
	4cm/1$^1\!/_2$ inches thick	16–18 mins / DH & IM	160F/71C
		(sear 10 mins DH, then 6–8 mins IM)	
	5cm/2 inches thick	20–24 mins / DH & IM	160F/71C
		(sear 10 mins DH, then 10–14 mins IM)	
thick rump tip or rump steak	450–900g/1–2lb	12–15 mins / DM	160F/71C
brisket	2.25–2.75kg/5–6lb	2$^1\!/_2$–3 hours / IM	160F/71C
boneless sirloin roast	1.75–2.75kg/4–6lb	1–1$^1\!/_2$ hours / IM	160F/71C
hamburger	2cm/$^3\!/_4$ inch thick	8–10 mins / DM	160F/71C
veal chop	2.5cm/1 inch thick	10–12 mins / DM	160F/71C

Type of lamb	Thickness or weight	Cooking time/method	Internal temp.
chop: loin, rib or chump	2.5cm/1 inch thick	8–12 mins / DM	160F/71C
leg of lamb steak	2.5cm/1 inch thick	10–12 mins / DM	160F/71C
rack of lamb	675g/1$^1\!/_2$lb	25–35 mins / DM	160F/71C
leg of lamb (boneless/rolled)	2.25–2.75kg/6–7lb	2$^1\!/_2$ hours / IM	160F/71C

Type of pork	Thickness or weight	Cooking time/method	Internal temp.
chop: rib, loin or shoulder	2cm/$^3\!/_4$ inch thick	10–14 mins / DM	160F/71C
	3cm/1$^1\!/_2$ inches thick	14–18 mins /DH & IM	160F/71C
		(sear 8 mins DH, then 6–10 mins IM)	
loin roast	1.5–2.25kg/3–5lb	1$^1\!/_4$–1$^3\!/_4$ hours / IM	160F/71C
spareribs	1.5–1.75kg/3–4lb	1$^1\!/_2$–2 hours / IM	160F/71C
loin chop (boneless)	2cm/$^3\!/_4$ inch thick	10–12 mins / DM	160F/71C
tenderloin (pork steak)	350–450g/12oz–1lb	25–30 mins / IM	160F/71C
sausage		25–30 mins / IM	160F/71C

1 tablespoon olive oil

1 small onion, chopped

2 red chillies, deseeded and chopped

3 tablespoons light soy sauce

1 tablespoon muscovado or brown sugar

1 lime, juice only

1 teaspoon curry paste

150g/5oz boneless skinless chicken breast

150g/5oz sirloin steak

150g/5oz pork tenderloin

Peanut sauce

1 tablespoon vegetable or peanut oil

1 garlic clove, finely crushed

1 teaspoon lemon grass, finely chopped

5 tablespoons crunchy peanut butter

150ml/¼ pint coconut milk

1 lime, juice only

1 teaspoon muscovado or brown sugar

1 teaspoon chilli powder

oil, for brushing

Mixed satays with peanut sauce

Gas	Direct/High heat	✹ ✹
Charcoal	Direct	
Prep time	40 minutes + 1 hour marinating	
Grilling time	6–8 minutes	Serves 4

1 Soak twelve bamboo skewers in cold water for 30 minutes. Heat the olive oil in a small frying pan and cook the onion and chilli for 3–4 minutes until softened. Remove from the heat and add the soy sauce, sugar, lime juice and curry paste. Put aside to cool.

2 Cut the chicken, sirloin steak and pork tenderloin each into four strips. Put into a non-metallic bowl and pour over the marinade. Toss well and marinate, covered, for 1 hour in the refrigerator.

3 To make the **peanut sauce**: Heat the oil in a saucepan and cook the garlic and lemon grass for 2 minutes until softened. Add the peanut butter, coconut milk, lime juice, chilli powder and sugar; simmer gently for 2–3 minutes until thickened. Keep warm.

4 Remove the strips of chicken and meat from the marinade and thread onto the skewers. Discard marinade. Brush the meat with a little oil. Barbecue over Direct High heat for 6–8 minutes on both sides, turning once. Serve with the warm peanut sauce.

Classic hamburgers in toasted sesame buns

675g/1½lb lean beef mince
2 garlic cloves, crushed
½ onion, coarsely grated
1 tablespoon
 Worcestershire sauce
225g/8oz Cheddar cheese,
 thinly sliced (optional)
salt and pepper
4 sesame hamburger buns
 or crusty rolls, split
sliced onion, sliced tomato,
 lettuce, mayonnaise,
 mustard, ketchup and/or
 cucumber relish, to serve

Gas	Direct/Medium heat
Charcoal	Direct
Prep time	10 minutes
Grilling time	12–16 minutes

Serves 4

1 In a large bowl, mix together the beef mince, garlic, onion, Worcestershire sauce and plenty of seasoning. Divide the mixture into four parts and shape into burgers.

2 Barbecue the shaped burgers over Direct Medium heat for 12–16 minutes, turning once until cooked through. For cheeseburgers, top the hamburgers with the cheese for the last 2–3 minutes of grilling time. Arrange the hamburger buns or rolls cut side down around the burgers for the last 2–3 minutes of grilling time to toast.

3 To serve, put one hamburger onto one half of each bun, add the topping of your choice, and place the remaining half bun on top.

Steak tortilla wraps with Mexican side dips

175ml/6fl oz lime juice
  (about 6 limes)
150ml/¼ pint vegetable
  juice
½ onion, finely chopped
1 tablespoon fresh parsley,
  chopped
2 garlic cloves, finely
  chopped
salt and freshly ground
  black pepper
675g/1½lb rump tip or
  rump steak
2 red peppers, deseeded
  and thinly sliced
1 large onion, thinly sliced
1 tablespoon olive oil
twelve 20cm/8 inch flour
  tortillas
tomato salsa, to serve
guacamole, to serve

Gas	Direct/Medium heat	✳ ✳
Charcoal	Direct	
Prep time	20 minutes + 3–4 hrs marinating	
Grilling time	10–19 minutes	Serves 6

1 Put the lime juice, vegetable juice, onion, parsley and garlic into a bowl and mix well. Put the steak into a non–metallic dish and pour over the marinade. Chill for 3–4 hours, turning the meat occasionally.

2 Meanwhile, cut a 45cm/18 inch square piece of heavy tin foil. Place the peppers and onion in the centre of the foil. Drizzle with the olive oil and season well. Bring the edges of the foil together and seal in the vegetables, to form a loose parcel.

3 Remove the steak from the marinade, reserving the marinade. Barbecue the meat over Direct Medium heat, 10–15 minutes for rare or 15–19 minutes for medium rare, turning once. Brush with the reserved marinade halfway through cooking time. Place the vegetable parcels on the cooking grate and cook for 12–14 minutes or until just tender.

4 Remove the steak from the grill and allow to rest for five minutes before slicing thinly. Meanwhile, wrap the tortillas in tin foil. Place on the cooking grate for 5 minutes, turning once to heat through.

5 Serve the sliced meat in tortillas with peppers, onions, salsa and guacamole on the side.

Pepper-crusted steaks with brandy cream sauce

3 tablespoons black
 peppercorns
4 sirloin steaks, about
 225g/8oz each in weight

Brandy cream sauce
1 tablespoon vegetable oil
1 onion or shallot, finely
 chopped
1 small garlic clove, crushed
2 tablespoons brandy
300 ml/½ pint good quality
 beef stock
6 tablespoons crème
 fraiche
salt and freshly ground
 black pepper
oil, for brushing

Gas	Direct/High heat
Charcoal	Direct
Prep time	10 minutes
Grilling time	8 minutes

✳ ✳ ✳

Serves 4

1 Put the peppercorns into a mortar and pestle and coarsely grind. Trim any excess fat from the steaks. Spill the crushed peppercorns onto a sheet of greaseproof paper and spread out. Press one side of each steak onto the peppercorns and shake off excess. Repeat with all the steaks until the peppercorns are used up.

2 To make the **brandy cream sauce**: Heat the oil in a small saucepan. Add the onion (or shallot) and garlic and cook over a gentle heat for 2–3 minutes until softened, then pour in the brandy, ignite and cook until flames subside. Add the beef stock and cook for a further 10–12 minutes until reduced to about 3½fl oz/100ml. Add the crème fraiche and cook for 5 minutes until very slightly thickened. Season well and keep warm.

3 Brush the steaks with a little oil and barbecue over Direct High heat for 8 minutes, turning once, for medium doneness. For well done, add 2–3 minutes each side. Serve with the hot brandy cream sauce.

Steak sandwich with Santa Maria sauce

1 tablespoon coarsely
 ground black pepper
2 garlic cloves, crushed
1 teaspoon mustard powder
1 teaspoon paprika
pinch cayenne pepper
1 kg/2½lb piece rump steak
 or rump tip, 5cm/2in thick

Santa Maria sauce
1 tablespoon olive oil
1 red onion, finely chopped
1 clove garlic, chopped
120ml/4fl oz chicken stock
4 tablespoons ketchup
4 tablespoons brown sauce
1 tablespoon fresh parsley,
 chopped
1 tablespoon
 Worcestershire sauce
1½ teaspoons ground
 coffee

French bread, to serve
oak/mesquite/hickory chips
 soaked for 30 minutes
 before grilling

Gas	Direct & Indirect/Medium heat
Charcoal	Direct & Indirect
Prep time	10 minutes + 4–24 hrs marinating
Grilling time	12–20 minutes

Serves 4

1 Put the black pepper, garlic, mustard, paprika and cayenne into a bowl and mix well. Rub the mixture into the surface of the meat, cover with cling film and chill for 4 hours or up to 24 hours.

2 Meanwhile, to prepare the **Santa Maria sauce**: Heat the olive oil in a saucepan, add the onion and garlic and fry gently for 3–4 minutes until softened. Add the chicken stock, ketchup, brown sauce, parsley, Worcestershire sauce, ground coffee and black pepper and bring to the boil. Simmer gently, stirring occasionally, until reduced to about 300ml/10fl oz. Pour into a food processor or blender and purée. Leave to cool, cover and chill until required but allow it to return to room temperature before serving.

3 Follow the grill's instructions for using wood chips (wood smoke enhances the flavour of the steak). Sear the steak over Direct Medium heat for 5 minutes, turning once. Finish over Indirect Medium heat, 8–10 minutes for rare, 10–13 minutes for medium, and 13–15 minutes for well done, turning once. Allow the meat to sit for 5 minutes before slicing. Sandwich the sliced meat and spoonfuls of the sauce between chunks of French bread and serve warm or at room temperature.

Barbecued pork with hot pepper vinegar sauce

2 tablespoons paprika

1 tablespoon light soft
brown sugar

1 tablespoon chilli powder

1 tablespoon ground cumin

1 tablespoon caster sugar

1½ teaspoons coarsely
ground black pepper

2 teaspoons salt

2kg/4½lb boneless pork
shoulder

Hot pepper vinegar sauce

175ml/6fl oz cider vinegar

175ml/6fl oz white wine
vinegar

2 tablespoons caster sugar

½ teaspoon chilli flakes

½–1 teaspoon Tabasco

salt and freshly ground
black pepper

16 hamburger buns or
crusty bread

coleslaw, to serve (optional)

Gas	Indirect/Medium heat	✳ ✳
Charcoal	Indirect	
Prep time	5 minutes	
Grilling time	3–4 hours	

Serves 8

1 Put the paprika, soft brown sugar, chilli powder, cumin, caster sugar, black pepper and salt into a small bowl and mix well. Rub the mixture all over the pork shoulder, pressing it well into the surface. Re-roll the pork and tie tightly with string at regular intervals around the meat.

2 Place the pork on the cooking grate and barbecue over Indirect Medium heat for 3–4 hours, turning regularly, until very tender. Remove meat from the grill, cover and allow to rest for 10 minutes.

3 Meanwhile, prepare the **hot pepper vinegar sauce**: put the cider and wine vinegars, caster sugar, chilli flakes and Tabasco into a saucepan. Bring to the boil, simmer for 10 minutes until reduced by about one third, season to taste and put aside, but keep warm.

4 Shred, chop or pull the pork into pieces using two forks. In a bowl, mix the shredded pork well with the hot pepper vinegar sauce. Serve the pork in the buns or bread with coleslaw (if using).

Buffalo-style ribs with blue cheese dressing

50ml/2fl oz cider vinegar

50ml/2fl oz olive oil

50ml/2fl oz Worcestershire
sauce

2–3 tablespoons chilli
sauce, to taste

1 tablespoon soft dark
brown sugar

1.5 kg/3 –3½lb pork back
ribs, in one piece

Blue cheese dressing

50ml/2fl oz mayonnaise

50ml/2fl oz soured cream

50g/2oz blue cheese, finely
crumbled

1 garlic clove, finely
chopped

½ teaspoon Worcestershire
sauce

1–2 tablespoons milk

salt and freshly ground
black pepper

Gas	Indirect/Medium heat	
Charcoal	Indirect	
Prep time	10 minutes + 4 hours marinating	
Grilling time	30–35 minutes	Serves 4

1 Put the vinegar, olive oil, Worcestershire sauce, chilli sauce and brown sugar into a small bowl and whisk together. Put the ribs into a large non–metallic dish, pour over the marinade and turn the ribs to coat. Cover the dish with cling film and chill for at least 4 hours or overnight, turning the ribs occasionally to distribute the marinade.

2 Meanwhile, to prepare the **blue cheese dressing**: Put the mayonnaise, soured cream, blue cheese, garlic and Worcestershire sauce into a small bowl and mix well. Add a little milk if the dressing is too thick. Season and chill until required.

3 Remove the ribs from the marinade and put the marinade into a small saucepan. Bring to the boil and boil hard for 1 minute, remove and set aside.

4 Place the ribs on the cooking grate bone side down (or use a rib rack) and barbecue over Indirect Medium heat for 30–35 minutes, turning once and brushing with the boiled marinade, until tender. Allow them to sit for 5 minutes before cutting into individual ribs and serving with the blue cheese dressing.

Grilled pork shoulder with spicy herb rub

1½ tablespoons paprika

1 tablespoon ground coriander

1 tablespoon lemon rind, finely grated

1 tablespoon dried marjoram

2 teaspoons garlic powder

1 teaspoon salt

¾ teaspoon freshly ground pepper

½ teaspoon ground cumin

¼ teaspoon caraway seeds, crushed

¼ teaspoon ground cinnamon

8 boneless pork shoulder steaks, cut ¾-inch thick (about 175g/6oz each)

Gas	Indirect/Medium heat	☀
Charcoal	Indirect	
Prep time	10 minutes	
Grilling time	10 minutes	Serves 8

1 In a small bowl combine the paprika, coriander, lemon rind, marjoram, garlic powder, salt, pepper, cumin, caraway seeds and cinnamon. Rub the herb mixture on both sides of the steaks, pressing into the surface.

2 Barbecue the steaks on the cooking grate over Indirect Medium heat for 10 minutes for medium cooked steaks, or 12–14 minutes for well done. Turn the steaks once halfway through grilling time.

Bratwurst rolls with soused red cabbage

375g/12oz red cabbage

1 onion

2 tablespoons sunflower oil

2 garlic cloves, crushed

$\frac{1}{2}$ tablespoon caraway
  seeds

120ml/4fl oz cider vinegar

2 tablespoons soft brown
  sugar

salt and freshly ground
  black pepper

6 bratwurst sausages

oil, for brushing

6 hot dog buns, split

hot mustard, to serve

Gas	Direct/Medium heat
Charcoal	Direct
Prep time	45 minutes
Grilling time	16–18 minutes

Serves 6

1 Using a sharp knife or a food processor, very finely shred the red cabbage and onion. Heat the oil in a large saucepan and add the cabbage, onion and garlic and stir-fry for 5–6 minutes, until softened.

2 Add the caraway seeds and stir-fry for a further 1–2 minutes. Add the vinegar, brown sugar and seasoning, bring to the boil, then reduce heat, cover and cook for 25 minutes until very soft. Turn off heat and leave aside to cool completely.

3 Lightly brush the sausages with oil and barbecue over Direct Medium heat for 16–18 minutes, turning once, until tender.

4 Spread each bun or roll with a little mustard, then fill with the soused red cabbage, top with a sausage and serve.

Char-sui pork with plum sauce

Char-sui marinade

4 tablespoons black treacle

2 tablespoons dark soy sauce

3 tablespoons dry sherry

3 pork tenderloins, each weighing about 375–450g/12oz–1lb

Plum sauce

675g/1½lb fresh plums

10 whole cloves

1 star anise

2 small dried chillies

250g/9oz brown sugar

1 teaspoon salt

2.5cm/1 inch piece fresh ginger, finely chopped

350ml/12fl oz white wine vinegar

oil, for brushing

Gas	Indirect/Medium heat	☀ ☀
Charcoal	Indirect	
Prep time	50 minutes + 4 hours marinating	
Grilling time	30 minutes	Serves 6

1 To make the **char-sui marinade**: Put the treacle, soy sauce and sherry into a small saucepan and stir over a gentle heat until well combined. Put aside to cool.

2 Trim the pork tenderloins of any excess fat and put into a large shallow dish. Pour over the marinade, turning the pork to make sure it is completely coated in the sauce. Cover and put into the refrigerator to marinate for 4 hours.

3 To make the **plum sauce**: Cut the plums in half and remove the stones. Crack the stones with a hammer and tie in a piece of muslin. In a second piece of muslin, tie the cloves, star anise and chillies. Put the two muslin bags into a large saucepan with the plums, sugar, salt, ginger and vinegar.

4 Bring the pan slowly to the boil until the sugar has dissolved, then simmer for 20 minutes until the plums are very soft. Remove the muslin bags and squeeze them over the pan. Boil vigorously for a further 5–10 minutes until thickened. Leave to cool (the sauce will thicken more when it's cooler).

5 Remove the tenderloins from the marinade and barbecue over Indirect Medium heat for 30 minutes. Slice the tenderloins and serve hot or cold with the plum sauce and noodles if liked.

Whole roast ham with orange apricot glaze

**1.5–2.25kg/3½–5lb cooked
boneless ham joint
whole cloves, to decorate**

Orange apricot glaze

**90g/3½oz apricot preserve
50ml/2fl oz orange juice
2 tablespoons soy sauce
½ lemon, juice only**

Gas	Indirect/Medium heat	✳ ✳
Charcoal	Indirect	
Prep time	5 minutes	
Grilling time	1½–2 hours	Serves 8–10

1 Using a sharp knife cut off the outer skin of the ham leaving a thick layer of fat. Score the fat of the ham, making diagonal cuts about 2.5cm/1 inch apart, to give a diamond pattern. Insert a whole clove in the centre of each diamond.

2 To make the **orange apricot glaze**: Mix together the apricot preserve, orange juice, soy sauce and lemon juice and then set aside.

3 Barbecue the ham over Indirect Medium heat for 1½–2 hours. During the last 15 minutes of cooking time, brush the ham all over with the glaze. Remove from the grill and leave to stand for 15 minutes before cutting.

4 Just before serving, heat the remaining glaze and brush the ham all over with more glaze.

Lamb rib chops with ginger & port

300ml/½ pint chicken stock

50ml/2fl oz ketchup

50ml/2fl oz tomato purée

1 small onion, finely
chopped

1 celery stalk, finely
chopped

50ml/2fl oz port

2 tablespoons honey

1 tablespoon fresh ginger,
grated

1 tablespoon brown sauce

1 tablespoon balsamic
vinegar

1 tablespoon
Worcestershire sauce

2 teaspoons chilli powder

2 teaspoons mustard
powder

2 teaspoons soft light brown
sugar

8 lamb rib chops

Gas	Direct/Medium heat
Charcoal	Direct
Prep time	5 minutes
Grilling time	7–17 minutes

Serves 4

1 Put the chicken stock, ketchup, tomato purée, onion, celery, port, honey, ginger, brown sauce, balsamic vinegar, Worcestershire sauce, chilli powder, mustard powder and brown sugar into a saucepan. Bring to the boil and simmer uncovered for 1 hour, stirring occasionally until sauce is thickened. Pour into a food processor or blender and blend until smooth. Leave to cool then chill until required. The sauce can be made up to 3 days in advance and stored in the refrigerator.

2 Barbecue the lamb chops over Direct Medium heat, 7–9 minutes for rare, 10–13 minutes for medium rare or 14–17 minutes for well done, turning once during cooking. Brush each side with the sauce for the last 2 minutes of grilling time. Remove chops from the grill and allow to rest for 3–4 minutes. Meanwhile, heat any remaining sauce and serve with the chops.

Rosemary veal chops with mushroom relish

2 tablespoons olive oil

1 tablespoon fresh rosemary,
 finely chopped

2 cloves garlic, finely chopped

½ lemon, grated rind only

½ teaspoon sea salt

4 veal rib chops, about
 2.5cm/1 inch in thickness

Mushroom relish

1 onion

225g/8oz fresh large shitake
 mushrooms

2 tablespoons olive oil

salt and freshly ground black
 pepper

1 small red tomato, seeded
 and diced

1 small yellow tomato, seeded
 and diced

1 tablespoon fresh thyme,
 chopped

2 teaspoons sherry vinegar

1 tablespoon extra virgin
 olive oil

1 tablespoon fresh parsley,
 chopped

Gas	Direct/Medium heat	❋ ❋
Charcoal	Direct	
Prep time	15 minutes	
Grilling time	25 minutes	Serves 4

1 In a small bowl, mix the olive oil, rosemary, garlic, grated lemon rind and salt. Brush the mixture over both sides of the veal chops, cover and chill while you prepare the grilled mushrooms.

2 To prepare the **mushroom relish**: Slice the onion into thick rings and put into a bowl with the shitake mushrooms and the olive oil. Toss gently to coat and season well. Grill the mushrooms and onions over Direct Medium heat, for 10 minutes, turning once, until tender and golden. Cool and chop roughly. Transfer to a serving bowl and add the tomatoes, thyme, sherry vinegar, olive oil and parsley. Toss well and check seasoning then set aside.

3 Remove the veal chops from the marinade and grill over Direct Medium heat for 12–15 minutes, turning once. They should be slightly pink in the centre.

4 Allow the veal chops to rest for 5–10 minutes, then serve with the grilled mushroom relish.

Vegetables & vegetarian

For a long time the barbecue had been the domain of the carnivore with the occasional piece of fish or a stray corn on the cob making an appearance. Today vegetables and vegetarian food are in demand by everyone – vegetables have become an essential part of our diet and grilling is a great way to prepare them. Most vegetables can be grilled in no time, provide a kaleidoscope of colour and offer good flavours and texture. Vegetarian dishes are surprisingly quick to prepare and simple to cook.

Most vegetables can be grilled on the barbecue with few exceptions. Larger vegetables such as red and green peppers or onions can be grilled as they come, placed directly on the cooking grate and then turned with tongs. Smaller cuts of vegetables, or indeed small vegetables like mushrooms, are best skewered to make turning easier and quicker. Vegetables should be lightly brushed with olive oil before grilling to prevent them from sticking to the cooking grate. If you are grilling vegetables alongside marinated meats or fish, consider brushing the vegetables with the same marinade. Unless otherwise specified, all vegetables should be turned once halfway through grilling time.

Vegetable kebabs

Vegetables most suitable for kebabs:
■ Button mushrooms, left whole ■ Peppers, cut into bite size pieces ■ Onions, cut into wedges ■ Courgettes, cut into thick slices ■ New potatoes, pre-cooked ■ Small or baby leeks, cut into lengths ■ Baby aubergines, cut in half ■ Small artichokes, pre-cooked and cut in half ■ Patty pans and baby squashes ■ Cherry tomatoes, skewered on their own and cooked briefly.

Type of vegetable	Cooking time/method
artichoke, globe	
whole	8–10 mins / DM
	(steam 20–25 mins; cut in half and grill)
asparagus, whole, trimmed	6–8 mins / DM
aubergine	
1cm/^{1}/$_2$ inch slices	8–10 mins / DM
halved	12–15 mins / DM
corn	
husked	10–12 mins / DM
in husk	25–30 mins / DM
courgette	
1cm/^{1}/$_2$ inch slices	6–8 mins / DM
halved	6–10 mins / DM
fennel	
5mm/^{1}/$_4$ inch slices	10–12 mins / DM
garlic, whole	45–60 mins / IM
leek, whole	14–16 mins / DM
mushroom	
shiitake or button	8–10 mins / DM
portobello	12–15 mins / DM
onion	
whole (do not peel)	45–50 mins / IM
peeled and halved	35–40 mins / IM
1cm/^{1}/$_2$ inch slices	8–12 mins / DM
spring onion, whole, trimmed	3–4 mins / DM

Type of vegetable	Cooking time/method
pepper	
whole	10–12 mins / DM
halved or quartered	6–8 mins / DM
potato	
whole	45–60 mins / IM
1cm/^{1}/$_2$ inch slices	14–16 mins / DM
new, halved	20–25 mins / DM
squash	
acorn 450g/1lb	40–45 mins / IM
butternut 900g/2lb	50–55 mins / IM
spaghetti 1.5kg/3lb	1^1/$_4$–1^1/$_2$ hours / IM
sweet potato	
5mm/^{1}/$_4$ inch slices	8–10 mins / DM
tomato	
halved	6–8 mins / DM
1cm/^{1}/$_2$ inch slices	2–4 mins / DM
whole	8–10 mins / DM
cherry, whole	2–4 mins / DM
plum, halved	6–8 mins / DM

The tables above are general guidelines rather than firm rules, and you should adapt your cooking times depending on the type and thickness of the vegetables you are barbecuing. These times are for crisp, tender vegetables.

Aubergine rolls with goat cheese & raita

2 aubergines

4 tablespoons olive oil, for brushing

175g/6oz goat cheese

3 tablespoons fresh sage, chopped

Raita

11oz/300g natural yoghurt

2 garlic cloves, crushed

4 tablespoons fresh mint, chopped

Gas	Direct/Medium heat	✳ ✳
Charcoal	Direct	
Prep time	20 minutes	
Grilling time	6 minutes	**Serves 8**

1 Soak 16 cocktail sticks in cold water for 30 minutes. Using a sharp knife top and tail the aubergines and cut each lengthways into eight slices. Brush each slice with oil on both sides. Season well. Barbecue over Direct Medium heat for 6 minutes, turning once, until tender. Put aside to cool.

2 Meanwhile, to make the **raita**: Put the yoghurt into a bowl and stir in the garlic and mint. Season well and chill until required. The raita can also be prepared in advance and kept chilled.

3 Cut the goat cheese into 16 pieces. Lay a piece of goat cheese on top of a slice of aubergine and scatter with a little chopped sage. Roll up and secure with a cocktail stick.

4 Barbecue the aubergine rolls over Indirect Low heat for 4 minutes, turning once.

5 Serve the warm aubergine rolls accompanied by the bowl of raita for dipping.

Bruschetta with tomatoes & anchovies

6 small plum tomatoes

2 tablespoons olive oil

6 x 1 inch thick slices of
baguette

1 large garlic clove

2 tablespoons tapenade or
black olive paste

6 large basil leaves

12 fresh or canned anchovy
fillets

freshly ground black pepper

olive oil, for drizzling

Gas	Direct/Medium heat	
Charcoal	Direct	
Prep time	15 minutes	
Grilling time	5–6 minutes	Serves 6

1 Cut the plum tomatoes in quarters and brush with a little oil. Barbecue over Direct Medium heat for 5–6 minutes, cut side up, until skin is slightly charred. Remove and put aside. Barbecue the bread slices over Direct Medium heat for 2–3 minutes, turning once until just toasted, and remove from the grill.

2 Immediately rub each toast slice with the garlic clove. Divide the tapenade between the bruschettas and top each with 2 tomato halves, a basil leaf and 2 anchovy fillets. Season with a little freshly ground black pepper. Drizzle with a little extra olive oil.

Hand-cut French fries with spicy ketchup

Spicy ketchup

150ml/¼ pint ketchup

1 tablespoon chilli sauce

2 teaspoons balsamic vinegar

900g/2lb potatoes, unpeeled

2 tablespoons olive oil

2 large garlic cloves, finely chopped

salt and freshly ground black pepper

Gas	Direct/Medium heat	☀
Charcoal	Direct	
Prep time	10 minutes	
Grilling time	10–12 minutes	Serves 4

1 To make the **spicy ketchup**: Put the ketchup, chilli sauce and vinegar into a small bowl, mix well and set aside.

2 Cut the potatoes in half then cut each half into four wedges or chunks. Put the olive oil, garlic and seasoning into a large bowl and mix well. Add the potato chunks and toss well until evenly coated.

3 Place the potato wedges on the grill, being careful not to let them drop through the grate. Barbecue over Direct Medium heat for 10–12 minutes, turning once, until golden brown on both sides. For extra crispness, open the lid during the last 2 minutes of grilling time. Serve hot with the spicy ketchup.

Corn on the cob

4 ears of corn with husks still attached

115g/4oz butter, softened

Jerk sauce

2 onions, chopped

2 garlic cloves, crushed

4 tablespoons lime juice

2 tablespoons dark molasses

2 tablespoons soy sauce

2 tablespoons fresh ginger, chopped

2 jalapeno chillies, deseeded and chopped

½ teaspoon ground cinnamon

¼ teaspoon ground allspice

¼ teaspoon ground nutmeg

6 ears of corn, husks removed

Chilli & coriander butter

115g/4oz butter, softened

1 red chilli, deseeded and finely chopped

1 tablespoon fresh coriander, chopped

Gas	Indirect/Medium heat	
Charcoal	Indirect	*
Prep time	10 minutes + soaking	
Grill time	20 minutes	Serves 4

1 Soak the corn in their husks in plenty of cold water for 30 minutes.

2 Remove corn and shake to get rid of excess water. Gently peel back husks without tearing the cob then remove and discard the silk. Smear the corn with butter and fold the husks back around the corn. Tie with cotton thread around the top to enclose.

3 Arrange corn on cooking grate and barbecue over Indirect Medium heat for 20–30 minutes until tender.

Corn with jerk sauce

Put all the sauce ingredients into a food processor and blend until finely chopped. Put each ear of husked corn on a large sheet of foil and spoon over the jerk sauce. Wrap the foil around the corn and sauce and barbecue over Indirect Medium heat for 15–20 minutes until tender.

Corn with chilli & coriander butter

Beat together the butter, chilli and coriander, use in place of the butter and continue as for top recipe.

Classic pizza Margarita-style

Pizza dough

**2 teaspoons easy blend
dried yeast**
1 teaspoon sugar
350g/12oz plain flour
1 teaspoon salt
200ml/7fl oz warm water
1–2 tablespoons olive oil

Topping

2 tablespoons olive oil
**1 small onion, finely
chopped**
1 garlic clove, crushed
½ teaspoon dried oregano
**600g/21oz can chopped
plum tomatoes**
2 teaspoons caster sugar
olive oil, for brushing
**225g/8oz buffalo mozzarella,
sliced and patted dry with
kitchen paper**
large bunch basil leaves

Gas	Direct/Medium heat	☀ ☀
Charcoal	Direct	
Prep time	40 minutes + resting	
Grilling time	8 minutes	Serves 4

1 To make the **pizza dough**: Mix the yeast, sugar, flour and salt in a large bowl. Make a well in the centre, add the warm water and olive oil and mix well into a dough. Knead the dough lightly on a floured surface until smooth. Put into a clean bowl, cover and leave to rise in a warm place until doubled in size.

2 Meanwhile, to make the **topping**: Heat the oil in a saucepan, sauté the onion and garlic for 2–3 minutes until softened, then add the oregano and tomatoes and cover and simmer for 10 minutes. Remove lid, add sugar and seasoning and cook uncovered for a further 10 minutes until the sauce is thickened.

3 Knead the dough again for a few minutes. Divide the dough in two and roll each piece into a circle, 25cm/10 inch in diameter. Brush both sides of each base with olive oil and slide the bases onto two baking trays.

4 Using long-handled tongs, slide the bases, onto the cooking grate and barbecue over Direct Medium heat for 2–3 minutes until the grill marks are visible. Slide back onto the baking sheet and turn the base so the grilled side is facing up.

5 Divide the tomato sauce between each crust and spread evenly with the back of a spoon, arranging the sliced

mozzarella on top. Slide the pizzas back onto the cooking grate and barbecue for 3–4 minutes, until cheese is melted.

6 Remove from the heat and top each pizza with a handful of basil leaves. Serve half a pizza per person.

Stuffed tomatoes with salsa verde

400g/14oz can cannellini
   beans, drained and rinsed
1 tablespoon sun-dried
   tomato paste
dash of Tabasco
50g/2oz fresh breadcrumbs
275g/10oz field mushrooms
2 tablespoons olive oil
1 onion, finely chopped
salt and freshly ground
   black pepper
3 tablespoons fresh parsley,
   chopped
12 large tomatoes
oil, for brushing

Salsa verde
3 tablespoons chopped
   fresh parsley
1 tablespoon fresh mint,
   chopped
3 tablespoons capers
1 garlic clove, crushed
1 tablespoon Dijon mustard
½ lemon, juice only
120ml/4fl oz extra virgin
   olive oil

Gas	Indirect/Medium heat	❋ ❋
Charcoal	Indirect	
Prep time	35 minutes	
Grilling time	8–10 minutes	Serves 6

1 Put the cannellini beans into a bowl and roughly mash to break up slightly. Add the tomato paste, Tabasco and fresh breadcrumbs and mix well.

2 Cut the mushrooms into pieces and put into a food processor. Blend until finely chopped and almost paste like. Heat the olive oil in a large frying pan and fry the onion for 6–7 minutes until very soft. Stir in the mushrooms and cook for a further 10 minutes, stirring occasionally until all the liquid has evaporated. Stir into the bean mixture and season. Stir in the parsley and put aside.

3 Cut the top quarter off the tomatoes and put aside. Scoop out the tomato pulp and discard. Season the empty tomatoes. Spoon the bean and mushroom mixture into each. Replace tops.

4 Brush each tomato with a little oil and barbecue over Indirect Medium heat for 8–10 minutes until softened and the filling is hot.

5 Meanwhile, put all the ingredients for the **salsa verde** into a food processor and blend quickly to make a thick paste with a coarse texture. Season well and serve with the hot tomatoes.

Roasted peppers with goat cheese & couscous

100g/4oz quick cook
  couscous
300ml/½ pint hot vegetable
  stock
25g/1oz butter
1 tablespoon fresh parsley,
  chopped
2 garlic cloves, crushed
16 black olives, roughly
  chopped
salt and freshly ground
  black pepper
4 large red peppers
4 small tomatoes
225g/8oz goat cheese
olive oil, for brushing

Gas	Direct/Medium heat	✳
Charcoal	Direct	
Prep time	35 minutes	
Grilling time	10 minutes	Serves 4

1 Put the couscous into a bowl and pour over the hot vegetable stock. Leave to soak for five minutes until the stock is absorbed and the couscous has softened. Add the butter, parsley, garlic, olives and seasoning and stir through with a fork.

2 Cut the peppers in half and remove and discard the seeds and white membrane. Cut the tomatoes in half and put one half into each pepper half. Spoon the couscous mixture around the tomatoes.

3 Cut the goat's cheese into eight slices and put a slice in the middle of each pepper.

4 Brush the outside of the peppers with olive oil. Barbecue over Direct Medium heat for 8–10 minutes until peppers are just tender and slightly scorched. Serve with salad.

Halloumi kebabs with spicy peanut sauce

12 baby new potatoes
2 garlic cloves
375g/12oz Halloumi cheese
8 chestnut mushrooms
8 bay leaves
oil, for brushing
salt and freshly ground
  black pepper

Spicy peanut sauce
115g/4oz crunchy peanut
  butter
3 tablespoons sesame oil
1 red chilli, deseeded and
  chopped
1 garlic clove, crushed
1 tablespoon sweet chilli
  sauce
6 tablespoons warm
  vegetable stock
2 teaspoons soft light brown
  sugar
2 teaspoons dark soy sauce
1 tablespoon lemon juice

Gas	Direct/Medium heat	☀ ☀
Charcoal	Direct	
Prep time	45 minutes	
Grilling time	10 minutes	Serves 4

1 Put the potatoes into a saucepan of water, bring to the boil and cook for 15–20 minutes until tender. Drain and leave to cool completely.

2 Cut the two garlic cloves into thin slivers. With the tip of a sharp knife make incisions into the potatoes and insert a few slivers of garlic into each potato.

3 Cut the Halloumi cheese into 12 even sized pieces. Skewer the garlic potatoes, cheese, mushrooms and bay leaves onto 4 skewers. Brush with oil and season well. Put aside.

4 To make the **spicy peanut sauce**: Melt the peanut butter in a bowl, sitting over a saucepan of simmering water. Heat the sesame oil in a small saucepan, add the chilli and cook for 1 minute to soften. Beat into the warm peanut butter with the garlic, chilli sauce, vegetable stock, sugar, soy sauce and lemon juice and heat through. Keep warm.

5 Barbecue the kebabs over Direct Medium heat for 10 minutes, turning once until vegetables are tender and cheese is golden. Divide the kebabs between 4 plates and drizzle with the warm spicy peanut sauce.

Rustic sandwich filled with grilled vegetables

2 red peppers, halved,
deseeded and quartered

4 medium sized flat
mushrooms

1 aubergine, cut into
1cm/$\frac{1}{2}$inch slices

50ml/2fl oz olive oil

salt and freshly ground
black pepper

2 tablespoons balsamic
vinegar

115g/4oz mascarpone
cheese

4 fresh ciabatta or other
rustic bread rolls

fresh basil sprigs, to serve

Gas	Direct/Medium heat	☀
Charcoal	Direct	
Prep time	10 minutes	
Grilling time	13 minutes	Serves 4

1 Brush the pepper quarters, mushrooms and aubergine slices with the olive oil. Barbecue the peppers over Direct Medium heat for 2–3 minutes.

2 Place the mushrooms and aubergine on the grill with the peppers and continue grilling for 8–10 minutes, turning occasionally, until all the vegetables are tender.

3 Put the vegetables into a large bowl, season and drizzle with the balsamic vinegar. Leave aside.

4 Split the rolls and toast each side on the grill. Spread the bottom half of each roll with the mascarpone cheese and top with the warm grilled vegetables and sprigs of basil. Replace the top of the bun and serve warm.

Chargrilled asparagus salad with Parmesan

24 asparagus spears
oil, for brushing
3 tablespoons olive oil
2 tablespoons balsamic
  vinegar
salt and freshly ground
  black pepper
175g/6oz rocket leaves
a large handful fresh basil
  leaves
75g/3oz Parmesan cheese

Gas	Direct/Medium heat	✳
Charcoal	Direct	
Prep time	15 minutes	
Grilling time	5–6 minutes	Serves 4

1 Trim the woody ends from the asparagus spears. Brush the asparagus with oil and lay the asparagus on the cooking grate, grilling over Direct Medium heat for 5–6 minutes, turning once, until marked by the grill. Leave aside to cool, then slice into pieces.

2 Whisk the olive oil, balsamic vinegar and seasoning. Toss with the rocket, basil leaves and asparagus spears.

3 Just before serving the salad drizzle balsamic dressing over and top with shavings of Parmesan cheese.

Mediterranean salad with peppers & croutons

oil for brushing
2 red peppers
2 green peppers
1 large bunch spring onions,
   trimmed
1 small loaf white bread
8 tablespoons olive oil
20 black olives
675g/1lb tomatoes
12 anchovy fillets drained
   and chopped
75g/3oz baby spinach
   leaves
2 garlic cloves, crushed
1 tablespoon Dijon mustard
2 tablespoons white wine
   vinegar
salt and freshly ground
   black pepper

Gas	Direct/Medium heat	☀
Charcoal	Direct	
Prep time	20 minutes	
Grilling time	15 minutes	Serves 6

1 Brush the red and green peppers with oil. Barbecue them over Direct Medium heat for 10–15 minutes, turning occasionally, until blackened and charred. Add the spring onions and barbecue for a further 4–5 minutes, turning once.

2 Put the hot peppers into a large bowl and cover with cling film and leave until cold. Cut the onions into lengths and put into a large bowl. When the peppers are cold remove the skins and seeds, cut the peppers into strips and add to the spring onions.

3 Remove the crusts from the loaf of bread and cut the white bread into neat cubes about 2cm/¾ inch. Heat 4 tablespoons oil in a large frying pan and add the cubed bread and cook for 5–6 minutes tossing occasionally until golden all over. Drain on kitchen paper and cool.

4 Cut the tomatoes into wedges and put into the bowl with the pepper strips and onions. Add the anchovy fillets and spinach leaves and toss well.

5 Whisk the garlic, Dijon mustard, vinegar, seasoning and the remaining olive oil together. Drizzle the dressing over the salad. Scatter with the croutons.

Desserts

Hot sunny days and cool balmy evenings are accompanied by the desire for sharp zingy seasonal berries, crisp sweet meringues and cool melting ice cream. Luckily, delicious grilled fare can include a host of tempting summer desserts from mini pavlovas with honeyed plums to seared strawberry sundaes.

Grilling fruits is a great way to bring out their best qualities – the sugars rise to the surface and caramelise, giving off wonderful aromas and a special flavour that can be enjoyed alone or paired with cakes, ice-creams or sauces. Even baked desserts usually associated with indoors get a look in; try the cherry and almond crumbles which can bake unattended, while the host and guests enjoy the main course.

Barbecued fruits are a wonderfully fresh way to finish a barbecue. Most soft fruits and some hard fruits such as apples and pears can be barbecued, but the most popular tend to be the tropical fruits such as pineapple, banana and mango.

Try a simple dessert of grilled fresh fruit drizzled with a little honey or topped with some ice cream if you can't face following a recipe. Something as simple as this can still make a decadent dessert to end any barbecue meal.

Fruit kebabs

This is a fun and incredibly easy way to serve a selection of fruit. Cut fruit into similar size pieces. Use wooden or bamboo skewers, as moist fruit spins around on smooth metal skewers. Soak the skewers in cold water first for at least 30 minutes to avoid burning. Barbecue kebabs over Direct Medium heat for 6–10 minutes, turning once. Brush kebabs with a mixture of liquid honey and lime juice halfway through grilling time.

Type of fruit	Cooking time/method
Apple	
whole	35–40 mins / IM
½ inch thick slices	4–6 mins / DM
Apricot	
halved, pit removed	6–8 mins / DM
Banana	
halved lengthwise	6–8 mins / DM
Cantaloupe	
wedges	6–8 mins / DM
Nectarine	
halved lengthwise, pit removed	8–10 mins / DM
Peach	
halved lengthwise, pit removed	8–10 minutes / DM
Pear	
halved lengthwise	10–12 mins / DM
Pineapple	
peeled and cored, ½ inch slices or 1 inch wedges	5–10 mins / DM
Strawberry	4–5 mins / DM

Note: Grilling times for fruit will depend on ripeness

Whatever fruit you intend to use, always clean the cooking grate well after cooking savoury foods. Brush your chosen fruit lightly with melted butter or a light, neutral vegetable oil to ensure it doesn't stick to the grill. It is important to remember that fruit only needs to be grilled long enough to caramelise their natural sugars.

Pavlova with honey-seared plums

4 egg whites
pinch of salt
225g/8oz caster sugar
2 teaspoons cornflour
1 teaspoon white wine
 vinegar
250g/9oz mascarpone
 cheese
300ml/½ pint double cream
2 tablespoons caster sugar
9 ripe plums
1 tablespoon liquid honey

Gas	Indirect/Medium heat	✻ ✻
Charcoal	Indirect	
Prep time	2 hours	
Grilling time	5–6 minutes	Serves 6

1 Preheat the oven to 180°C/350°F/Gas 4. Lightly grease two large baking trays and line with non-stick greaseproof paper. Put aside.

2 In a clean bowl whisk the egg whites with the salt until soft peaks form. Gradually whisk in the caster sugar, a little at a time, to give a stiff glossy meringue mixture. Whisk in the cornflour and vinegar. Take a large spoonful of the meringue and spoon onto one of the lined baking trays and form into a round. Make a slight dent in the centre with the back of the spoon to give a nest shape. Repeat to make six in all, spaced well apart. Bake for 5 minutes then reduce oven temperature to 150°C/275°F/Gas 1 and bake for a further 1 hour 15 minutes. Leave to cool on the baking trays.

3 Meanwhile, in a clean bowl, whisk the mascarpone cheese until softened. In a separate bowl whisk half the double cream and caster sugar until soft peaks form. Fold into the softened mascarpone with the remaining cream until smooth. Cover and chill until required.

4 Soak six short bamboo skewers in cold water for at least 30 minutes. Cut the plums in half and remove stones. Thread three halves onto each skewer, cutting the skewer to size if

necessary. Brush with the honey. Barbecue over Indirect Medium heat for 5–6 minutes until just softened.

5 Peel the meringues off the paper and spoon the mascarpone cream into each. Serve each meringue with a warm skewer of grilled plums.

Green-peppered pineapple with orange caramel

1 teaspoon green
  peppercorns in brine,
  drained and roughly
  chopped
4 thick slices fresh
  pineapple
2 teaspoons caster sugar

Orange caramel
125 g/4 oz granulated sugar
1 orange, rind and juice
50ml/2fl oz single cream

good quality vanilla ice
  cream, to serve

Gas	Direct/Medium heat	✹ ✹
Charcoal	Direct	
Prep time	5 minutes	
Grilling time	6–7 minutes	Serves 4

1 Rub the peppercorns into both sides of each pineapple slice. Sprinkle one side of each slice with the sugar.

2 Place pineapple slices, sugar side down, in the centre of the cooking grate. Barbecue over Direct Medium heat for 6–7 minutes or until browned.

3 Meanwhile, to make the **orange caramel**: Put the granulated sugar and orange rind into a small saucepan with 2 tablespoons cold water, and heat gently until dissolved. Bring to the boil and cook for 4–5 minutes until a golden caramel colour. Remove from the heat and stir in the orange juice and the cream then return to the heat and cook gently, stirring until smooth. Leave aside.

4 To serve, put the grilled pineapple slices into four serving dishes and pour over the warm orange caramel and top with some vanilla ice cream.

Caramelised bananas with coconut & orange

oil, for brushing

7 tablespoons caster sugar

2 tablespoons desiccated coconut

grated rind of 1 orange, reserve fruit for the juice

300ml/½ pint double cream

2 tablespoons rum

6 large bananas

Gas	Direct/High heat	✳
Charcoal	Direct	
Prep time	30 minutes	
Grilling time	5 minutes	Serves 6

1 Brush a baking tray with a little oil and put aside. In a saucepan put 6 tablespoons of the caster sugar with 2 tablespoons cold water. Dissolve the sugar slowly, then bring to the boil and cook for 6–8 minutes until it turns a golden caramel colour. Remove from the heat and stir in the coconut and orange rind.

2 Pour caramel onto the oiled baking tray and put aside for 10 minutes to set. When set hard break into pieces and put into a food processor and grind to a powder. Put aside.

3 Meanwhile whip the cream with the remaining caster sugar and rum until soft peaks form. Chill until required.

4 Cut the bananas in half lengthways. Squeeze a little juice from the orange over the banana halves and then sprinkle the surface of each half with the caramel and coconut. Barbecue skin side down over Direct Medium heat for 5 minutes until the caramel mixture is melted and golden. Serve warm with the rum cream. Decorate with orange zest.

Grilled figs Spanish style

1 vanilla bean

115g/4oz fresh, soft goat
  cheese

300ml/½ pint double cream

2 tablespoons caster sugar

12 fresh figs

50g/2oz good quality plain
  chocolate

Gas	Direct/Low heat
Charcoal	Direct
Prep time	20 minutes
Grilling time	6–8 minutes

✹ ✹

Serves 6

1 With the tip of a sharp knife split open the vanilla bean and scrape out the seeds. Put the seeds into a bowl with the goat cheese and beat well. In a clean bowl whip the double cream with the caster sugar to soft peaks then fold into the vanilla flavoured goat cheese. Chill until required.

2 Using a small sharp knife, cut a cross in the figs about three quarters way through the fruit and open out like a flower.

3 Cut the chocolate into twelve small nuggets. Bury a nugget of chocolate in the centre of each fig, then barbecue the figs over Direct Low heat for 6–8 minutes until chocolate is melted and figs are soft.

4 Serve two hot figs per person on a serving plate with a scoop of the vanilla goat's cream.

Peach parcels with amaretti-filled centres

115g/4oz amaretti biscuits
75g/3oz flaked almonds
50g/2oz light muscovado
  sugar
75g/3oz butter, diced
1 lemon, grated rind and
  juice
1 large egg yolk, beaten
6 ripe peaches

Gas	Indirect/High heat	☀
Charcoal	Indirect	
Prep time	20 minutes	
Grilling time	15 minutes	Serves 6

1 Crush the amaretti biscuits roughly and put into a large bowl. Add the almonds, muscovado sugar, butter and lemon rind. Work the mixture with your fingertips until the mixture resembles coarse breadcrumbs. Add the egg yolk and mix well until mixture is just sticking together.

2 Cut the peaches in half then remove the stones and discard. Dip each peach half in lemon juice. Divide the filling amongst the peach halves, pressing down lightly to fill the cavity.

3 Take six large squares of extra thick tin foil about 20cm/ 8 inch square. Put two filled peach halves on each square and bring edges together and scrunch together to loosely seal in peaches. Barbecue over Indirect High heat for 15 minutes until the peaches are soft and the filling is sizzling. Serve hot with scoops of vanilla ice cream.

Kirsch-soaked cherries with almond crumble

675g/1½lb fresh cherries,
  or two 400g/14oz cans
  cherries in syrup
2 tablespoons Kirsch
1 orange, grated rind only

Crumble topping
200g/7oz plain flour
150g/5oz butter, diced
75g/3oz flaked almonds
150g/6oz brown sugar

crème fraiche, for garnish

Gas	Indirect/Medium heat	☀ ☀
Charcoal	Indirect	
Prep time	35 minutes	
Grilling time	20 minutes	Serves 6

1 If using fresh cherries, stone the cherries first. Put into a large bowl and pour over the Kirsch. Add the orange rind and mix well. If using tinned cherries in syrup, drain very well and mix with the Kirsch and orange rind and put aside.

2 To make the **crumble topping**: put the flour into a large bowl with the butter. Using your fingertips, rub in the butter until the mixture resembles rough breadcrumbs, then stir in the almonds and brown sugar.

3 Divide the cherries between six small heatproof dishes, or large ramekins, or place them in one large shallow pie dish. Top with the crumble mixture. Place on the cooking grate and barbecue over Indirect Medium heat for 20 minutes until the top is golden and the cherry mixture is bubbling. Leave to cool slightly before serving with spoonfuls of crème fraiche.

Seared strawberry & vanilla sundae

900g/2lb strawberries
4 tablespoons icing sugar
3 teaspoons balsamic
  vinegar
150ml/¼ pint double cream
3 tablespoons chopped nuts
good quality vanilla ice
  cream, to serve

Gas	Indirect /Medium heat	
Charcoal	Indirect	
Prep time	20 minutes	
Grilling time	6 minutes	Serves 4

1 Put half the strawberries, 2 tablespoons of icing sugar and balsamic vinegar into a food processor or blender and blend to a smooth sauce. Chill until required.

2 Whip the double cream and 1 tablespoon icing sugar to stiff peaks and chill. Toast the nuts under a pre-heated grill until golden brown. Put aside to cool.

3 Thread the remaining strawberries onto two or three metal skewers (this makes them easier to turn) and dust with the remaining icing sugar. Barbecue over Indirect Medium heat for 6 minutes, turning once, until soft and marked with the grill.

4 Spoon a little sauce into the bottom of four sundae glasses and top with two scoops of vanilla ice cream. Take the grilled strawberries off the skewers and divide between the glasses, reserving four for decoration. Spoon the whipped cream on top. Pour over more strawberry sauce and decorate with chopped nuts and reserved strawberries.

Index